Instructor's Resource Manual

DISCOVERING THE AMERICAN PAST
A LOOK AT THE EVIDENCE
Fifth Edition

William Bruce Wheeler

University of Tennessee

Susan D. Becker

University of Tennessee, Emerita

HOUGHTON MIFFLIN COMPANY   BOSTON   NEW YORK

Editor-in-Chief: Jean Woy
Associate Editor: Leah Strauss
Editorial Assistant: Christian Downey
Manufacturing Manager: Florence Cadran
Senior Marketing Manager: Sandra McGuire

Printed in the U.S.A.

ISBN: 0-618-10226-4

123456789-B&B-05 04 03 02 01

Contents

Volume II

Preface

"We study history," educator Diane Ravitch has said, "because it provides us with the knowledge, vocabulary, idioms, and language in which to make connections between the past, the present and the future." Like many other contemporary observers, Ravitch believes that the study of history should encourage independence of thought. When unprepared high school and college students encounter overly detailed, boring textbook presentations and standardized tests, their interest and natural curiosity about are history are stifled. Questions about why something happened—and why it *matters* that something happened—are submerged in "laundry lists of disconnected facts."[1]

Of course, it did not have to be so. In the 1870s, Henry Adams, then an assistant professor of history at his alma mater, Harvard College, offered a seminar in which the professor introduced a problem and students went into the primary source evidence in search of "answers":

> The boys worked like rabbits, and dug holes all over the field of archaic society; no difficulty stopped them; unknown languages yielded before their attack, and customary law became as familiar as the police court; undoubtedly they learned . . . to chase an idea like a hare, through as dense a thicket of obscure facts. . . . As pedagogy, nothing could be more triumphant.[2]

Adams modestly claimed that he adopted this teaching style only because the lecture system "suited Adams not at all" and also because he didn't know enough about the past to write an adequate set of lecture notes. At the same time,

---

[1] Diane Ravitch, "Obstacles to Teaching History Today," excerpts from a speech to the New Jersey Council for History Education on March 15, 2001, *History Matters!* 13 (June 2001): 1, 6–7.

[2] Henry Adams, *The Education of Henry Adams* (Boston: Houghton Mifflin Co., 1918), p. 303.

however, he confessed that he "wanted to teach his students something not wholly useless."[3] He did.

As with its four preceding editions, the fifth edition of *Discovering the American Past: A Look at the Evidence* is a book written in the spirit of Henry Adams's stimulating classes, which many of his students later reported were the high points of their college experience. Students will like its problem-solving approach and the opportunity to explore the past the same way historians do. Because many instructors believe that students learn more and retain that knowledge longer if they approach American history as active learners, this book can become a valuable tool for strengthening students' critical thinking skills.

Discovering the American Past is a problems-oriented collection of primary sources. Those sources are clustered around a set of problems that students are required to solve as active learners.[4] The primary sources are both traditional and nontraditional: letters, memoirs, newspaper articles, court decisions, speeches, trial manuscripts, prescriptive literature, and biographical sketches are inter-mixed with works of art, statistics, maps, music lyrics, political cartoons, photo-graphs, architectural plans, advertisements, posters, and oral history.

The nature of *Discovering the American Past* is such that the instructor's role will be greater than that of a lecturer, although lectures are crucial to setting up these problems, providing factual information, and offering interpretive frame-works. The instructor will also become a resource person and a guide, in the best sense of those terms. Students will need the assistance of their instructors even more, as students and instructors work together to solve historical problems and learn skills.

Format

The *Instructor's Resource Manual* for *Discovering the American Past*, fifth edition, is dramatically different from the usual manuals that are filled for the most part with skeletal chapter summaries and test items. While we try to create as much flexibility as possible for instructors and encourage them to be as innovative as they dare, the *Instructor's Resource Manual* offers a running commentary on each section of the chapters found in the students' text, based on our use of this material in our own classrooms.

For the section "The Problem" we state the central questions the students are required to answer, as well as the content objectives and skills objectives for that chapter. The "Background" section places the problem in its historical context and serves as an introduction to the problem being studied. In "The Method" section,

---

[3] Ibid., p. 302.

[4] For a good discussion of active learning, see Chet Meyers and Thomas B. Jones, *Promoting Active Learning: Strategies for the College Classroom* (San Francisco: Jossey-Bass, 1993).

we introduce the methodology that students are to use when dealing with that problem's evidence. "The Evidence" section summarizes the particular pieces of evidence the students will be using. Here we try to clarify not only what to do but how to do it. In the section "Questions Students Often Ask," we answer some of the most often asked questions that students have raised (remember that active learners ask a lot of questions).

For the section in the students' text entitled "Epilogue," we have given instructors some suggestions for evaluation. There are no true-false or multiple-choice tests in the *Instructor's Resource Manual,* but rather some ideas for a variety of evaluations that can be tailored to the skills and content mastery that the instructor thinks are most important for his or her own students. Ideally, every student would do every exercise, but time limitations or grading load might make this impossible. If so, students might work in pairs or small groups. Still another method is to cluster some of the problems into broad chronological packages. For example, the first four problems in Volume I (First Encounters, Anne Hutchinson, Rhythms of Colonial Life, and the Boston Massacre) might be clustered, with one-fourth of the class each doing one of the problems and reporting on it to their classmates. There are various ways in which student learning can be evaluated: out-of-class writing exercises, student journals, quizzes, essay examination questions, graded discussions, oral reports, and simulations such as role playing and mock debates. The options are limited only by the instructor's ingenuity, time, and energy!

Finally, there is a section entitled "For Further Reading" that lists some books the instructor might want to consult as preparation for guiding students in the various problems.

Responses to the Text

Our teaching experiences and other instructors' responses to the four previous editions indicate that working with primary evidence can interest and motivate American history survey students in a variety of classroom situations. Small, self-contained courses provide a kind of ideal setting in which the instructor can most easily adjust the skills and content objectives of this book to the particular needs of his or her students. But many (perhaps too many) of us teach very large United States history survey courses. Sometimes we team-teach; sometimes we alternate discussion sections with large lecture sections; and frequently we rely upon graduate teaching assistants to help us. Because more of us are coping with this phenomenon today, we have written a separate section in this manual on teaching large classes in which we share more specifically some of the techniques and approaches we've used in our classes.

Most gratifying to us have been the students' reactions. Both of us—as well as colleagues who write us from across the nation—report students' enthusiasm with the *active learner* approach to American history. "This is the best course I've taken so far in college," said many students. "In this class, I get the opportunity to think for myself," others reported. "I actually look forward to coming to class," said a fair number. While we would dearly love to take credit for all of those wonderful evaluations, we understand (as instructors with over fifty combined years of classroom teaching) that our colleagues in the many colleges and universities where *Discovering the American Past* is used deserve most of the credit. And to them, this book is dedicated.

What's Different About *Discovering the American Past?* A Guide to Switching from the Fourth to the Fifth Edition

The changes for the fifth edition described below are the most specific and notice-able ones, the ones that will be most important to instructors in the process of writing a course syllabus or arranging lecture notes. There are many more general and pervasive changes as well. All the chapters from the fourth edition have been rethought, discussed, retested, and in many cases revised. All the bibliographic essays have been updated.

VOLUME I

Chapter 3   Rhythms of Colonial Life: The Statistics of Colonial Chesapeake Bay and Massachusetts Bay

This chapter has been rewritten and new evidence provided to allow students to *compare* colonial development in these two important areas of early settlement.

Chapter 6   Land, Growth, and Justice: The Removal of the Cherokees

The central question of this chapter has been recast and the evidence rearranged to make it easier for students to follow the arguments for and against Indian removal.

Chapter 9   Slavery and Territorial Expansion: The Wilmot Proviso Debate, February 1847

This is a new chapter that uses the debates over the expansion of slavery to highlight the increasing sectional conflict and unwillingness to compromise.

Chapter 11   Grant, Greeley, and the Popular Press: The Presidential Election of 1872

This is another new chapter. This problem focuses on the issues related to Reconstruction in the pivotal election of 1872. Political cartoons by Matt Morgan and Thomas Nast expose students to a different kind of visual evidence.

VOLUME II

Chapter 1   Grant, Greeley, and the Popular Press: The Presidential Election of 1872

Same as Volume I, Chapter 11.

Chapter 6   The "New" Women: Social Science Experts and the Redefinition of Women's Roles in the 1920s

This new chapter introduces students to the powerful influence of social scientists on the changing roles of women during the era.

Chapter 11   A Nation of Immigrants: The Fourth Wave in California

This is also a new problem; it emphasizes the importance of immigration as a theme in our history by analyzing the experiences of the most recent (post-1965) newcomers to California: Hispanics and Asians.

Using the Book in Large Classes

Recently, many universities (including our own) have increased class sizes and instituted large lecture sections without any opportunity for discussion. This was brought home to us most dramatically when each of us was assigned to teach a United States history survey course in a classroom that held 268 students, with no discussion sections. And yet we found that *Discovering the American Past* worked well in that setting too.

We laid out for the students at the beginning of each problem (chapter) our content and skills expectations (goals). We then divided the large classroom into groups of ten or so, assigning each group a chapter on which to work. Students in each group were expected to meet out of class to prepare a presentation for the rest of the students. For each chapter, we introduced the problem with a lecture that set the problem in its contextual framework and then asked that particular group of students to present the chapter to the class. Some were quite innovative: a simulation of the trial of Anne Hutchinson; a tour guide escorting the class through the 1904 St. Louis Exposition (complete with slides the students had made from the book); a debate between Wells, Washington, Turner, and Du Bois (with students taking those roles). Questions and comments were loud and plentiful. And students were *learning:* how to think critically, how to work in a group, how to organize a presentation, how to engage their fellow students, how to defend themselves against questions. They also *learn content,* and (based on test results) they *retain.*[1]

An increasing number of instructors of large classes have used the method of *pair problem solving* with *Discovering the American Past,* and with considerable success.[2] The instructor divides the class into many (sometimes dozens of) pairs of

[1]See Chet Meyers and Thomas B. Jones, *Promoting Active Learning: Strategies for the College Classroom* (San Francisco: Jossey-Bass, 1993).

[2]For an explanation of pair problem solving, see J. Lochhead and A. Whimbey, "Teaching Analytical Reasoning Through Thinking Aloud Pair Problem Solving," in J. E. Stice, ed., *Developing Critical Thinking and Problem-Solving Abilities* (San Francisco: Jossey-Bass, 1987).

students. The pairs then meet separately outside class. As one student listens, the other "talks through" the problem. Then the two students switch roles. Finally, they talk through the problem together. Pairs may be selected by the instructor to report their findings.

Yet another approach we have tried is to introduce *Discovering the American Past* as a kind of primer about how historians actually "*do*" history. This shifts the focus toward the kinds of evidence and methodologies that historians use. It also means that the instructor has to explain a bit more about "tests cases" or microcosms, limited generalizations, chains of evidence or linkages in arguments, and so forth. This approach very much emphasizes the problem-solving and critical thinking aspects of our work, and tends to privilege the skills objectives over the content objectives.

Of course, one of the best ways to use *Discovering the American Past* in large classes is to have the students regularly write out answers to questions, keep student journals, and so on. Instructors should be warned, however, that evaluating these written works might be impractical. On the other hand, many instructors believe that writing helps students clarify and organize their thoughts and that all out-of-class writing need not be evaluated (or "graded").

Whatever methods an instructor chooses to employ, *Discovering the American Past* can be used in a wide variety of classroom situations, among them the very large class.

VOLUME I

CHAPTER 1

First Encounters: The Confrontation Between Cortés and Montezuma (1519–1521)

Many years ago, when we were growing up in different areas of the United States, we both loved going to the movies on Saturday mornings or afternoons. We watched courageous frontiersmen, cowboys, and U.S. cavalrymen battle against— and usually defeat—their Indian foes, the chiefs of whom usually were played by white actors such as John Hodiak, Jeff Chandler, J. Carrol Naish, and Chuck Connors. In those films, Indians were referred to as "redskins," "savages," "aborigines," and so forth. As we wolfed down popcorn and guzzled soft drinks, little did we suspect that we were watching a collective image of Native Americans that was far from accurate and distinctly unhealthy.

Yet until relatively recently, historians have done little better, and calls for improvement by voices such as that of the fine historian James Axtell have been like cries in the wilderness. For traditional historians, perhaps the main problem was one of adequate sources. Like white women and African Americans, rarely were Native Americans permitted to speak with their own voices in traditional sources. We can count fewer than half a dozen confrontations between Europeans and Indians in the period prior to 1775 in which available sources record both sides of the confrontation.

For that reason alone, this chapter on the confrontation between the meager forces of Hernando Cortés and the Aztecs ruled by Montezuma is of particular value. Thanks to some courageous Roman Catholic priests, these Aztec sources were saved from Spanish destruction and spirited to Europe, and some of them were later returned to Mexico City. This chapter relies primarily on sources that found their way to Florence, Italy (the famous *Florentine Codex*).

The Problem

Content Objectives

1. To learn how European explorers and colonists perceived (or misperceived) the indigenous Native Americans and how the Indians perceived (or misperceived) Europeans

2. To learn how European perceptions shaped their attitudes and actions regarding Indians and how Indian perceptions shaped their attitudes and actions regarding Europeans

Skills Objectives

1. To be able to analyze primary source material (written accounts) so as to differentiate in that material the images being transmitted

2. To be able to use artistic representations as evidence and to discover the "messages" that works of art communicate

On a larger scale, ask your students to think about the following questions:

1. Why did Europeans and white Americans continue to view nonwhites as inferior? How has this prejudice continued to affect our thinking even today? (Do not neglect the Native American population here.)

2. How accurate or inaccurate were European perceptions of Indians? (You will have to help here.) Why did such inaccuracies exist, and why do they continue to exist?

3. When we speak of a melting pot in America, do we exclude Indians? If not, how are the Indians supposed to fit in?

Background

This section reviews how the peoples whom Columbus misnamed Indians got to North America, the long history of some of these peoples, and the diversity of Indian life at the time Europeans first encountered them. Of course, the various Indian groups had evolved to different stages of development, but the Europeans treated all the Indians the same way.

The rest of the Background section touches briefly on the Aztec empire and provides a biographical sketch of Cortés. You may have to reinforce the fact that the Aztecs in Tenochtitlán were at least as "civilized" (and possibly more so) as their European conquerors. Cortés and his soldiers were clearly exploiters who sexually abused the conquered women and appropriated Aztec property. Cortés himself, although married, fathered several children by conquered Aztec women. The Spanish *conquistadores* in the New World both expected and received large grants of land as well as Indian and African slave laborers to work the land.

The Method

As in subsequent chapters, the Method section introduces students to the types of evidence they will be examining and analyzing, sometimes asking leading questions about those types of evidence. In this chapter, students are given two types of evidence: (1) literary accounts written by Cortés and by Aztecs and (2) artistic representations by Europeans of Indians and by Indians of Europeans. Note that the European artists (for the most part) had not traveled to America or even seen an Indian, whereas the Aztec artists had seen Europeans firsthand.

It is important that you get your students to think in terms of images: How would the average European (with access to this evidence) have perceived Indians? We ask students to think of adjectives these types of evidence might suggest. Later, students can ruminate on the impact of these adjectives and images.

The Aztec chroniclers and artists were attempting to convey an image of Europeans. What was that image? How would that image have helped or hindered Indians who viewed those sources? Would it have made them firmer in their resistance? Or would it have given them a defeatist attitude?

The Evidence

There is little doubt that Cortés was prepared to see the host population as "savages," in spite of the fact that he described their dwellings and cities in complimentary terms. Note his description of the Indians' "ugly" adornments, such as earrings and nose rings. Cortés makes much of the Indians' religious ceremonies, including the use of incense (which also was burned in Roman Catholic churches) and human sacrifice (the Spanish Inquisition burned heretics at the stake). Doubtless the Aztec rituals of human sacrifice were both bloody and appalling, but note that Cortés's description of that practice is followed immediately by his use of those sacrifices as justification for conquering and Christianizing the Indians. Indeed, he even saw the Aztec religion as "in the service of the devil." Given that belief, Cortés offered a justification for the slaughter about which he boasts.

The Europeans' artistic renderings can be divided into two general groupings: generally hostile (Sources 2, 3, 5, 7, and 9) and patronizing (Sources 4, 6, and 8). As the students will see, both images ultimately had the same results. Ask your students to think of descriptive adjectives for each of the sources. For example, Sources 2, 3, 5, and 7 definitely portray Indians as bloodthirsty and scheming. Yet Sources 4, 6, and 8 portray a different image: innocent, childlike, accepting. As you work your way (and the students' way) through this evidence, ask them to concentrate on each work of art and its intended message.

As the *conquistadores* had misperceptions of Indians so also did the indigenous population initially have misperceptions of them. After the Aztecs' initial offers of friendship were rebuffed, Montezuma's representatives reported on the Spanish cannon, clothing (including armor), weapons, horses, skin color, food, and dogs. In one sense, that description sealed the Aztecs' fate, for unlike the European descriptions, the Indian descriptions were filled with awe and fear (note Montezuma's reaction, due only in part to the prophecy of the arrival of conquerors from the east). From then on, the account is a chronicle of Spanish barbarities; as for the artistic representations, Sources 11 and 12 deal with the initial meetings, and Sources 13 and 14 portray the slaughter.

Questions to Consider

As in subsequent chapters, these questions help students read and analyze the evidence. Many professors ask their students to read this section *before* examining the evidence because it offers several leading questions to help them "untangle" the evidence. This section is a walk-through of the evidence, so we ask our students to read the evidence and then, using this section, go back through it with these questions in mind. In subsequent chapters, students have to go through the Evidence section more than once.

Questions Students Often Ask

Is it true that the Europeans brought the practice of scalping to America?
There is no truth to that statement. Indeed, historian James Axtell asserts that this myth actually came into general circulation through an assertion made on a television program. However, Europeans did increase this practice by paying Indians for scalps (from Europeans' enemies, escaped slaves, and so forth).

How many Europeans actually saw the art depicting Native Americans?
Actually, a good number did, especially in the German states. Accounts and artistic representations of the New World became part of Europe's popular culture.

What diseases killed the Indians? Did Indians carry any diseases that affected Europeans?
Europeans communicated to the Indians smallpox, influenza, and dysentery, all of which were fatal because the Indians did not have the proper immune systems. From the Indians, Europeans contracted syphilis, which they brought back to the Old World.

How prevalent was cannibalism among the Indians?
Not very, although one part of the ritual of human sacrifice in Tenochtitlán did involve the symbolic cooking and eating of enemies' flesh. Some peoples

in the highlands of the Caribbean islands practiced cannibalism. It is interesting that students ask this question.

Those artists who actually saw Indians portrayed them as having large stomachs. Was this an accurate representation?
Probably, because of malnutrition.

Why didn't Indians wear more clothing?
Many Indians, especially in North America, did, covering themselves with deerskins, bearskins, and the pelts of other animals. Climate played a role, too. The major question (a turnaround) is why European artists depicted Indians as naked or seminaked.

Did all the Spanish conquerors portray the Aztecs the same as Cortés?
No. The most dramatic example of the conflicting view is that of Bartolomé de Las Casas, a Dominican priest who wrote extensively from America urging the Spanish monarchs to treat the Indians humanely. He was devastatingly critical of Cortés, whom he saw as a greedy adventurer.

Did Indians practice infanticide (killing newborns and children)?
Yes, but so did Europeans ("laying over").

Epilogue and Evaluation

The Epilogue section deals primarily with why Indians were so vulnerable to European intrusions. We especially stress disease, European technology, internal conflict among the Indians, Indian misperceptions of Europeans, and the Indians' destruction of their own ecology. The section concludes with a statement about racial and ethnic images, images that have proved ultimately destructive.

In this first chapter, we preferred not to evaluate students' written work. We show them the *format* of the course, make them feel at ease in discussing their ideas, and help them to believe in us (in such a course, trust is terribly important).

If, however, you want to evaluate students' understanding of this chapter, you might have them write an essay a mid-seventeenth-century European might have written if he or she had seen all the evidence. What the Indian was really like is a good subject.

On a larger note, ask your students to deal with racial stereotypes. How do people who have never seen an Indian get their ideas about Indians? How valid or invalid are these images? When images conflict, how do people choose which image they will accept?

For Further Reading

General studies of Native Americans before the European conquest include Alvin M. Josephy, Jr., *America in 1492: The World of the Indian Peoples Before the*

Arrival of Columbus (1991); Brian M. Fagan, *Kingdoms of Gold, Kingdoms of Jade: The Americas Before Columbus* (1991); and Gary Nash, *Red, White, and Black: The Peoples of Early North America* (3rd ed. 1992). David Carrasco has described the Aztec culture in *Montezuma's Mexico: Visions of the Aztec World* (1992) and *City of Sacrifice: The Aztec Empire and the Role of Violence in Civilization* (1999). There are two excellent, recently-published reference guides for South and Central American Indian life: *The Cambridge History of the Native Peoples of the Americas* (1996–1999), vol. II and *Mesoamerica*, and *The Oxford Encyclopedia of Mesoamerican Cultures*, 3 volumes (2000). Peter C. Mancall's review article, "The Age of Discovery," *Reviews in American History* 29 (March 1998): 26–53, offers a useful analysis of the difficulties inherent in the textual and visual source material which form the basis for our knowledge of sixteenth century encounters in the New World.

The impact of this contact between the Europeans and Native Americans has been the subject of many historical studies. Two of the best known are Alfred W. Crosby, *The Columbian Exchange: Biological and Cultural Consequences of 1492* (1972) and Herman J. Viola and Carolyn Margolis, *Seeds of Change: Five Hundred Years Since Columbus* (1991). Several studies debate the extent of the European impact on indigenous populations: Russell Thornton, *American Indian Holocaust and Survival: A Population History Since 1492* (1987); David Stannard, *American Holocaust: The Conquest of the New World* (1992); and David Henige, *Numbers from Nowhere: The American Indian Contact Population Debate* (1998). Elinor G. K. Melville's *A Plague of Sheep: Environmental Consequences of the Conquest of Mexico* (1994) focuses on the long-term changes in the indigenous ways of life.

Two additional recent interpretive works are Richard C. Trexler, *Sex and Conquest: Gendered Violence, Political Order and the European Conquest of the Americas* (1995); and Patricia Seed, *Ceremonies of Possession in Europe's Conquest of the New World, 1492–1640* (1995). For detailed, narrative overviews, see Ross Hassig's *War and Society in Ancient Mesoamerica* (1992) and *Mexico and the Spanish Conquest* (1994). Serge Gruzinski's *Painting the Conquest: The Mexican Indians and the European Renaissance* (1992) and *The Conquest of Mexico: The Incorporation of Indian Societies into the Western World, Sixteenth to Eighteenth Centuries* (1993) are also useful.

Additional primary sources may be found in Bernal Diaz Del Castillo, *The Discovery and Conquest of Mexico, 1517–1521*, edited and translated by Genaro Garcia and A. P. Maudslay (1956); Miguel Leon-Portilla, editor, *The Broken Spears: The Aztec Account of the Conquest of Mexico* (1962); Marvin Lunenfeld, editor, *Discovery, Invasion, Encounter* (1991); James Lockhart, editor and translator, *We People Here: Nahuatl Accounts of the Conquest of Mexico* (1993); Patricia de Fuentes, *The Conquistadors: First Person Accounts of the Conquest of Mexico* (1993); and Jill LePore, *Encounters in the New World: A History in Documents* (2000). A very well-chosen selection of documents with an excellent introduction is Stuart Schwartz's *Victors and Vanquished: Spanish and Nahua Views of the Conquest of Mexico* (2000).

CHAPTER 2

The Threat of Anne Hutchinson

In 1688, Puritan leader William Stoughton delivered an election-day sermon in Dorchester, Massachusetts Bay colony, that contained the following observation: "For many a day and year, even from our first beginnings, hath this word of the Lord been verified concerning us in this wilderness: the Lord hath said of New England, surely they are my people." The notion of being a "chosen people" with a special relationship to God through the covenant they believed God had made with them compelled the Puritans to deal harshly with those who threatened their special status, their unity, or, as they saw it, their determination to keep the covenant. It is in this light that the expulsion of Roger Williams, the execution of Quaker Mary Dyer, and even the Salem witchcraft trials, which, as historian John Demos showed, were the most sensational of such activities, can be viewed. The trial of Anne Hutchinson is the window through which we examine and analyze Puritan society and beliefs.

The Problem

Content Objectives

1. To understand Puritanism in Massachusetts Bay colony

2. To understand how seventeenth-century Puritan thought explains Puritans' actions

3. To understand the nature of the threat Anne Hutchinson posed

4. To understand the Antinomian controversy that shook the colony from roughly 1636 to 1638

Skills Objectives

1. To be able to read for comprehension

2. To be able to identify and juxtapose main arguments and lines or reasoning found in primary source material

3. To be able to discuss those findings and express ideas in a classroom situation

On a larger scale, you may want to use the chapter to stimulate thought and discussion on one or more of the following questions:

1. To what extent can a community restrict the rights of individuals for the greater good of the community? Who determines that greater good? Are individualism and individual freedom modern notions?

2. Is freedom of religion a right that should supersede all other freedoms? To what extent does the community have the right to restrict religious freedom when that freedom becomes dangerous to the community? Did the Puritans practice freedom of religion as we know it? If not, why not?

There are other larger questions or issues that you might want to have students think about and discuss. The problem is flexible enough that you can bend it to your particular points or concerns. We use our lectures to provide the background and setting of a problem and to suggest the questions and issues of larger concern.

The Method

On the surface, the ability to read for comprehension and identify main lines of argument in selections are skills students should already possess when they begin tackling "The Threat of Anne Hutchinson." Unfortunately, this is not always the case. Used with care, however, this assignment can help build these skills and therefore enhance performance in later chapters.

To begin, we find it helpful to clarify the trends and events leading up to the Hutchinson trial, either in a lecture on Puritanism or in a class discussion of the introduction to the evidence (labeled "The Background"), which the students have read. This helps set students on fairly firm ground as they approach the evidence.

A few days before the chapter is to be discussed, we go over with students the first half page or so of the evidence. Through guided discussion, students learn to summarize each statement in their own words and to understand where the lines of argument are leading. We instruct our students to summarize the rest of the evidence on their own, suggesting that they take detailed notes as they go along. At times we even suggest that they place their notes in two columns: column 1 summarizes each passage, and column 2 contains the principal lines of argument. Those notes also are beneficial for later discussion.

Some instructors have found it helpful to ask for student volunteers to prepare oral presentations of the testimony. Hearing the language read out loud aids many students to understand the arguments and get a sense of the underlying tensions in the trial. Other instructors have students read the Questions to Consider section *before* looking at the evidence, so that they have more guidance in dealing with the unfamiliar language.

The Evidence

The first section of evidence contains a general argument between Winthrop and Hutchinson over the precise charges against her. A few students might consider this section as nit-picking, but students need to see Winthrop's and the other colonial authorities' determination to be rid of Hutchinson. Moreover, students can better appreciate Hutchinson's own style: intelligent, aggressive, and well-spoken.

The charge of breaking the fifth commandment (Honor thy father and thy mother) is confusing to some students. During discussion, we try to get students to think about the term *parents*. Did this term refer to Anne Hutchinson's actual parents? If not, did Winthrop mean the "fathers of the commonwealth"? The evidence seems to point in the latter direction.

The second section of the trial deals with the meetings Hutchinson held in her home. The issue of combined meetings of men and women is confusing, especially because Hutchinson denied she presided over combined meetings. Were such meetings specifically forbidden? Why was such a point made of them?

Finally, unable to crack Hutchinson's composure or get her to admit wrongdoing, an angry and exasperated Winthrop complained, "We are your judges, and not you ours." Students should note Winthrop's frustration and ill-concealed dislike of Hutchinson.

The next section, beginning with Deputy Governor Thomas Dudley's accusation, concerns the nature of what Hutchinson was preaching. You may have to help students understand the following difficult concepts: the difference between a covenant of grace and a covenant of works; why preaching a covenant of works was considered unacceptable to Puritans; and why criticizing ministers (all but Cotton) was so potentially dangerous. Students will recall much of this material from the chapter's introduction and/or from your introductory lecture or remarks.

Cotton's defense of Hutchinson was hardly what we would call strong. But many historians believe that she was more than holding her own until she told the General Court about her revelations. This action presents a real problem that students will need to discuss. Hutchinson must have known that admitting to revelations would be extremely damning to her case, yet she almost bragged about them. Why? Did she want to be expelled? Why?

After Hutchinson spoke of her revelations, the results were a foregone conclusion, if they had not been before.

Questions to Consider

The questions help students clarify the evidence they have read and understand the various reasons or a combination of reasons why Hutchinson was such a threat to Massachusetts Bay. The reasons—and there may well be others—are as follows:

1. Hutchinson was a threat to the community because she was subverting colonial order without having broken a specific law.

2. She was a threat to the community because she criticized the ministry and in so doing implied the ministers were in violation of the covenant.

3. She was a threat to the community because she violated the "place" assigned women.

Of course, all these reasons may be partly correct. But judging from the testimony, what principal threat did Hutchinson pose? Students should enjoy discussing this question.

Such a discussion also should bring out the central difficulty many students have with studying history: what is the "right" answer? We believe this problem should be confronted as quickly as possible, and "The Threat of Anne Hutchinson" is a good forum for doing so. Although there is no "right" answer, we want students to understand how historians use evidence to find the *most probable* answer to a problem. Why is there no right answer on which all historians can agree? We find that getting this problem out of the way at the beginning of the course helps the level of discussion later.

Questions Students Often Ask

Why didn't Anne Hutchinson's own minister (John Cotton) defend her more forcefully?

Cotton himself had come under attack earlier for preaching sermons that were too close in tone to those of the banished John Wheelwright. Given the conservative turn of the General Court and the reinstallation of Winthrop as governor, Cotton could have been in considerable trouble had he defended Hutchinson more forcefully.

Had Hutchinson ever experienced revelations before?

Yes. She claimed that in 1633 she had informed her family that a revelation from God told her to follow Cotton to New England.

If Hutchinson had kept quiet about her revelations, would she have been acquitted?

Writing in *American Heritage* (June 1974), historian Wellington Newcomb suggested that Hutchinson's critical mistake was speaking about her revelations. Numerous historians, including Edmund Morgan, agree with Newcomb. One must keep in mind, however, that Winthrop appears to have been determined to banish Hutchinson.

Except for her family, did anyone go to Rhode Island with Hutchinson?

After Hutchinson's conviction, her supporters were disfranchised. Indeed, there was some fear that these supporters would have revelations compelling them to kill Hutchinson's judges. When she was banished, Hutchinson was accompanied by approximately thirty families.

Why didn't Hutchinson stay in Rhode Island, an area known for its religious toleration?

There are several reasons. First, it is highly probable that Hutchinson, a person who believed she possessed the "true word," was interested not in religious toleration but in an orthodoxy with which she agreed. Second, Hutchinson's husband died in Rhode Island, and it appears that this also prompted her to leave. Third, one must remember that she migrated to a very sparsely settled area, all the better to practice her own brand of orthodox Puritanism.

Epilogue and Evaluation

The "Epilogue" puts the chapter back in its historical context. It is short and meant only to supplement your own work and the students' supplementary reading.

Besides the traditional written examination or quiz, student performance in "The Threat of Anne Hutchinson" can be evaluated in several ways. At times, we ask students to imagine that they are spectators at Hutchinson's trial and instruct them to write a letter to an imaginary relative or friend in England explaining the Hutchinson incident. This task lets us evaluate the extent to which the students have acquired a grasp of the main issues, the lines of argument in the trial, and the significance of the event.

For those who choose not to evaluate "The Threat of Anne Hutchinson" in writing, evaluating the discussion is an option. Some of our colleagues use a class session to simulate the trial. Students are assigned roles (the remainder act as a jury of sorts), and they re-create the trial. Our colleagues report that students are enthusiastic about this approach.

Of course, you have evaluated class discussions before, and your own method should work well with this chapter. We also use "The Threat of Anne Hutchinson" to identify reading, note-taking, and other problems that individual students may be having.

For Further Reading

The best brief introduction to the early history of Massachusetts Bay colony is still Edmund S. Morgan's lively *The Puritan Dilemma: The Story of John Winthrop* (1958). For an overview of Puritan thought, see Darren Staloff, *The Making of an American Thinking Class* (1998). For Puritan society, see Virginia

Anderson's *New England's Generation* (1991) which analyzes nearly seven-hundred English emigrants of the Great Migration and focuses on the critical phases in their lives during the 1630s. Economic aspects of Puritanism and the relationship between commerce and orthodox religion are examined in Mark Peterson, *The Price of Redemption: The Spiritual Economy of Puritan New England* (1997). Two excellent studies of popular religious beliefs in New England are David D. Hall's *Worlds of Wonder, Days of Judgment* (1989) and Richard Godbeer's *The Devil's Dominion* (1992).

In *Saints and Sectaries: Anne Hutchinson and the Antinomian Controversy in the Massachusetts Bay Colony* (1962), Emery Battis offers a sociopsychological interpretation of the Hutchinson trial and the events leading up to it. Seventeenth-century Puritan radicalism in general and its impact on the New England Way are the subjects of Philip F. Gura's *A Glimpse of Sion's Glory* (1984), while Timothy Hall's *Separating Church and State: Roger Williams and Religious Liberty* (1998) offers a careful analysis of Williams' dissent. Hall has also published the basic documentary history of this era's major dissenting movement, *The Antinomian Controversy* (2nd ed., 1990). In his revisionist article "New England and the Challenge of Heresy, 1630 to 1660: The Puritan Crisis in Transatlantic Perspective," *William and Mary Quarterly* (October 1981), pp. 624–660, Stephen Foster argues persuasively that Puritanism could tolerate and absorb more dissent, including antinomianism, than historians have previously believed.

Laura Thatcher Ulrich's *Goodwives: Image and Reality in the Lives of Women in Northern New England* (1982) is a very good, readable introduction to the activities and experiences of "ordinary" women by a Pulitzer Prize-winning historian. Several studies are relevant to the gender questions raised by Hutchinson's trial. John Winthrop's intense dislike for Anne Hutchinson is evident in Richard Dunn et al., *The Journal of John Winthrop, 1630–1649* (1996). In *A Search for Power: The "Weaker Sex" in Seventeenth Century New England* (1980), Lynn Koehler emphasizes the oppressiveness of male-dominated Puritan society and sees antinomianism as an outlet for Hutchinson, who was representative of the many rebellious and dangerous women who threatened the patriarchal authority. Literary scholar Jane Kamensky agrees, arguing in *Governing the Tongue: The Politics of Speech in Early New England* (1997) that failure to fit into the "norms of godly womanliness" put Hutchinson (unlike Roger Williams) outside the parameters of discourse about the covenant of grace. Lad Tobin, "A Radically Different Voice: Gender and Language in the Trials of Anne Hutchinson," *Early American Literature* 25 (1990): 253–270; and Marilyn Westerkamp, "Puritan Patriarchy and the Problem of Revelation," *Journal of Interdisciplinary History* 23 (1993): 571–595, also focus on the significance of gender with respect to heresy.

CHAPTER 3

Rhythms of Colonial Life: The Statistics of Colonial Chesapeake Bay and Massachusetts Bay

Approximately forty years ago American historians "discovered" statistical analysis and, as a result, computers. Taking their cues from the earlier *Annales* School of French historians, these students of American history began to explore limited geographical areas (a township, a county, for instance) in considerable depth in order to learn significantly more about groups of people who left little or no written records. Calling themselves "New Social" historians (to distinguish themselves from earlier social historians who took a more anthropological approach to peoples of the past), these men and women made important contributions to our understanding of American history.

No chronological period of American history benefited more from the work of these "New Social" historians than did the colonial period. Historians such as James Henretta, John Demos, Allan Kulikoff, Philip Greven, Kenneth Lockridge, Robert Gross, Paul Boyer, Stephen Nissenbaum, and many others deepened our understanding of the crucial trends of growth, change, and maturation that took place between settlement and the American Revolution. Using mostly demographic and economic statistics, these historians discovered many factors that shaped the lives of American colonists, including some trends and forces which the colonists themselves may not have been made aware of.

Current "New Social" history is neither new or so popular as it was in the 1960s and 1970s. And while an overarching "New Social" synthesis of the American colonial period that connected these fascinating town and county studies has not yet appeared (and, indeed, may never appear), the "New Social" historians provided an important foundation upon which to build other interpretations of the colonial era and even give us a fresh perspective of the lives of American colonists in the years prior to the American Revolution.[1]

---

[1]One excellent effort was James Henretta's *The Evolution of American Society, 1700–1815: An Interdisciplinary Analysis* (1973).

The Problem

Content Objectives

1. To understand the important trends of growth, change, and maturation as they occurred in colonial America between the time of settlement and the American Revolution

2. To understand the differences between the Chesapeake Bay and Massachusetts Bay colonies, the demographic and economic changes that took place in these colonies, and whether those changes were moving the Chesapeake Bay and Massachusetts Bay colonies closer together or further apart

3. To appreciate the role demographic and economic factors play in human affairs

4. To appreciate the fact that the history of any people is the history of *all* the people, not just the leaders

Skills Objectives

1. To be able to use demographic and economic material to study history and contemporary life.

2. To be able to interpret statistics and use them to construct a narrative

3. To be able to compare and contrast statistics from different places (in this case the Chesapeake Bay and Massachusetts Bay colonies)

On a larger scale, the chapter can be used to stimulate thought and discussion of one or more of the following questions:

1. To what extent is history the analysis of the forces over which people have comparatively little control? (This is a variation of the determinism versus free will argument.)

2. Do people fully understand the extent to which these forces influence their behavior? Do people perceive these forces in their lives?

3. How does ideology or collective mentality motivate individuals or groups? What are the relationships between demographic and economic forces and ideology?

You may want to use this problem to get students to think about a larger question that you have devised. We use an introductory lecture to set out all our objectives and the larger questions about which we want students to be thinking. We know that many of our students do think about such questions; our colleagues in other disciplines have reported that some students bring these questions into their other courses.

Background

Students easily visualize the settlements of the Chesapeake Bay and Massachusetts Bay colonies, in large part through mental pictures of John Smith, John Rolfe, Pocahontas, John Winthrow, Anne Hutchinson, and others. Similarly, students also readily recall Revolutionary leaders from those colonies such as Thomas Jefferson, Charles Carroll, Samuel Adams, and others. What students often *cannot* do, however, is see beyond the famous individuals to the typical men, women, and children of colonial America. Nor can they offer much understanding of what took place in those colonies in the century and a half between settlement and independence. Finally, students appear to be unable to compare and contrast these colonies in any significant ways. The Background section, therefore, offers a brief introduction to the colonization, growth, and change of Virginia, Maryland, and Massachusetts Bay upon which to build the forces and trends gleaned from the statistics.

The Method

About twenty years ago, when we began experimenting with using demographic and economic statistics in our classes, students exhibited much apprehension, insecurity, and even fear about statistics. But with time, these feelings diminished significantly. Personal computers and other innovations have made students more aware of statistics and somewhat less apprehensive about working with them. Yet some uneasiness still exists. Some students have never worked with statistics and feel uncomfortable doing so. They must overcome this obstacle before they can effectively answer the questions in this chapter. One method we use to deal with this obstacle is a personal data sheet. The student fills in the following information:

Age
Number of siblings
Birth order among siblings
Occupation of parents (or student's occupation)
Number of residences lived in during entire life to date
Educational level of parents
Approximate income of parents (or student's income)
Urban, rural, small town, etc. (population)
Age at which student had first unchaperoned date

Other students face a different and more challenging problem. Believing that statistics are "objective," these students feel that statistics can tell the whole story and with total accuracy. This attitude leads to a notion of historical inevitability, which we think is just as hazardous as a complete rejection of statistical evidence. Returning to the aggregated information from the class's personal data sheets, we ask the students what the statistics do *not* tell and, in some cases, *cannot* tell.

In the Method section of this chapter, students are introduced to the methods historians use to link quantitative data so they can examine and analyze the lives of the "ordinary" people of the colonial period. The section briefly sketches what kinds of records are collected, how they are aggregated and ordered, and what questions historians ask the data. Then students are instructed to examine each set of statistics in the Evidence section, asking three questions of each set:

1. What does the set measure?

2. How did what is being measured change over time?

3. Why did that change take place?

Students are told that they will find the answer to question 3 (the "why" question) in another statistical set. Once they find the answer, the students have established a linkage. They are instructed to repeat the process until all the sets are linked. Finally, they are told to answer the four central questions:

1. What were the *environmental* and *volitional* differences between the Chesapeake Bay and Massachusetts Bay colonies?

2. What *demographic* and *economic* changes took place in those colonies between roughly 1650 and 1750?

3. How might those changes have affected the respective colonists' thoughts, feelings, and behaviors?

4. Were demographic and economic changes moving the Chesapeake Bay and Massachusetts Bay colonies closer together or further apart?

During the past few years, we have recognized some good and bad tendencies in our students. One good tendency is that students attempt to complete any assignment given them by an instructor, no matter how daunting. A corresponding bad tendency is that they give up too easily and do not keep working. Those students reason that surely someone in the class will complete the assignment successfully and that the rest of the class can lean on him or her. Have you recognized similar tendencies in your students? If you have, then you know that you will be challenged to keep your students working even after their initial disappointments.

The Evidence

Sources 1 through 14 are statistical sets from the Chesapeake Bay colonies. Sources 25 through 27 are statistics from Massachusetts Bay. Where possible, we have arranged the statistical sets so that those from Chesapeake Bay and those from Massachusetts Bay follow the same format:

	Source Number	
Subject	Chesapeake Bay	Massachusetts Bay
Population growth	1–3	15–17
Survival rates	5–6	18
Age at Marriage	4, 5	22
Landholding	7	20
Division of Estates	11	21
Alternatives	12–14	24, 26–27

Other statistical sets do not have exactly corresponding sets for the other colony/colonies.

The first set of statistics, Sources 1 through 3, deal with population growth in Virginia and Maryland from roughly 1640 to 1770. The growth rates by decades might be compared to the growth rates of the students' hometowns. Almost immediately students will see that the growth rate for the white populations of Virginia and Maryland either declined or barely held steady, whereas the growth rates for the black populations remained comparatively high (see the ultimate results in Middlesex County, Source 3). Clearly both colonies were moving toward large plantation agriculture that increasingly used black slave labor rather than white indentured servants from Great Britain. Students should consult Sources 7 and 10 on the evolution of the plantation system.

Sources 4 through 7 often present students with something of a puzzle. Clearly the average age at first marriage for white females in Middlesex County was rising, from 18.1 in 1670–1679 to 22.0 in 1740–1749. An even more dramatic rise can be seen in Tidewater, Maryland. In Maryland, we can also see that the average completed family size was declining, and we might suppose that a similar trend was taking place in colonial Virginia as well. Students enjoy offering explanations for both phenomena (the "why" question), and many suppose that Chesapeake Bay planters were attempting to maintain their economic, social, and political positions by not dividing their landholdings among all male heirs (Source 11). Students also assert that sons without inheritance very likely would have to defer marriage until they could secure their own landholdings. Still others are able to connect these demographic choices with what appear to be increasingly difficult economic times (Sources 8 and 9), in which the price of tobacco generally was drifting lower while the value of goods imported from England continued to rise.

Thus, with a good deal of work, students are able to see that the Chesapeake Bay colonies by the mid-eighteenth century faced demographic and economic difficulties. Sources 12 through 14 demonstrate how many colonists chose to deal with those difficulties (by shifting from tobacco to wheat and/or by moving westward), *in addition to* altering age-at-marriage and inheritance patterns. Indeed, even as the American Revolution approached, whites in the Chesapeake Bay colonies faced equally daunting problems.

As your students worked through the first series of statistical sets (for the Chesapeake Bay colonies, Sources 1 through 14), they almost immediately confronted two major problems. The first major problem (see Sources 1 and 2 for good examples) is that statistics can show *general tendencies or trends* but cannot always explain exceptions to those tendencies or trends. In Source 2, for instance, the population growth rates for Maryland's white population *tended* to decline from the mid-seventeenth century to the mid-eighteenth century, while the black growth rates either increased or held steady. Yet there are numerous "blips" in both white and black population growth rates that cannot be explained by statistics alone—and in some cases cannot be satisfactorily explained at all.

The second major problem your students will confront is that of "missing" statistics. For example, in New England we have statistics on the average farm sizes (Source 20 for Concord, for instance), but comparable data for Virginia and Maryland is not available throughout the colonial period. But we *do* have data on the *number of slaves* on plantations, and we can substitute this information in place of actual acreage to show general tendencies (the percentage of large farms, or plantations, was increasing). Also, when your students approach the Massachusetts Bay statistics, they will see that population density figures for Concord and Andora are not available for all dates. Yet there are enough statistics to be able to see the *general tendency or trend.* Remind students that people in colonial times were not as statistically conscious as we are.

The Chesapeake Bay colonies and Massachusetts Bay were profoundly different in colonists' motives, governmental and social structures, and economic and labor systems. Moreover, both environmental and volitional differences appear to have been increasing, thus moving the Chesapeake Bay and Massachusetts Bay colonies further apart. And yet, students will recognize almost immediately that similar demographic and economic difficulties were being experienced in both regions: population growth (Sources 15 through 17), survival rates (Source 18), age at marriage and family size (Sources 22 and 23), division of estates (Source 21), economic choices (Sources 26 and 27). In terms of choices, Chesapeake planters shifted to wheat (Sources 12 and 13) while the Massachusetts economy was moving toward shipping (Source 26). Both regions embraced westward expansion as a "safety valve" (Sources 14 and 27). For Massachusetts, the other "safety valve" (if it could be called that) was Boston.

Thus students will recognize that economic and labor systems were moving the Chesapeake Bay and Massachusetts Bay colonies further apart. And yet, at the same time, they seem to have faced similar problems (population growth), adopted similar "solutions" (increased age at marriage, smaller families), attempted to alter their respective economies (wheat for the Chesapeake, shipping for the Massachusetts), and ultimately used westward expansion as a "safety valve." So are similar demographic and economic trends moving the two regions closer together or further apart? If students have worked through both series of statistics, the discussion should be stimulating. Moreover, it will give students a much better understanding of later forces in American history (westward expansion, the sectional crisis, the debate over the role of the federal government in the private economic sector, and so forth).

Questions to Consider

The questions lead the students step by step through the statistical sources without divulging too much. In this section, we also break the crust on the questions about the extent to which people are aware of demographic and economic forces and the extent to which some of their feelings may be redirected. You may not want to pursue the topic at this time—or at all.

Questions Students Often Ask

Why did planters in Virginia and Maryland embrace slavery rather than continue using indentured servants from Great Britain?

According to Edmund Morgan (*American Slavery, American Freedom*), once indentured servants began living long enough to be free of their contracts and become farmers themselves, the market became glutted with too much tobacco (see Source 8). Also servants and former indentured servants demanded political rights and participated in Bacon's Rebellion against Tidewater planters in 1676.

Why didn't the Chesapeake Bay colonies have any cities such as Boston to absorb the excess rural population?

One of the most important functions cities perform is the collection and distribution of goods. In the Chesapeake Bay colonies, merchants' representatives (called *supercargoes*) traveled by boat up the bay and rivers directly to the plantations to buy tobacco and deliver goods.

Were there any poor white people in the Chesapeake Bay colonies? You've talked mostly about planters.

Although large planter-slaveowners dominated the economic, social, and political life of the Chesapeake Bay colonies *and* their wealth and power were *increasing*, the majority of whites were small farmers. As one can see in Middlesex County (Source 3), whites were *leaving* in increasing numbers as the large plantation system became solidified. Competition with slave labor caused many to leave Virginia altogether.

Did only men inherit land in colonial America?

If there were males in the family, they inherited the land. Women received the estate's personal property (furniture, dishes, and so on). If there were no males in the family, women could inherit land, although when they married, the ownership automatically transferred to their husbands.

What kinds of jobs did single men and women obtain when they migrated to Boston?

Men often worked on the docks or in the ropewalks or shipyards. Women worked in inns or taverns, or as domestic servants.

If so many people were migrating to Boston, why didn't the town's population increase more?

Many people were moving out, too, usually to other seaboard towns and cities. Recall that Benjamin Franklin was born in Boston.

Where in Boston did the migrants live?

Many rented modest rooms near the docks or in the North End, near the mill pond. By 1800, the mill pond was so polluted that a group of inspectors reported dead animals floating along the top of the contaminated water.

In 1771, the richest 10 percent of Boston's population owned 63.4 percent of the town's taxable wealth. How does that compare with today?

According to the *Federal Reserve Bulletin* of September and December 1984, America's wealthiest 10 percent in 1983 owned 86 percent of the nation's individual net financial wealth. Moreover, it is commonly believed that the percentage has increased since then.

Could you say that demographic and economic problems were a factor in the colonists' rebellion against Britain?

Well, you *could* say that, but could you *prove* it? How would you go about proving it? One could prove that demographic and economic troubles contributed to Boston's reputation as being the "enfant terrible" of the New World. The Chesapeake Bay colonies would be more difficult.

Epilogue and Evaluation

The Epilogue briefly explores the myth of John Adams's thirteen clocks striking "together—a perfection of mechanism, which no artist had ever before effected." Thus students are cautioned not to try to assert that all colonists who supported the Patriot cause in the American Revolution did so for the same reasons. Indeed, many New Englanders feared that those from the Chesapeake Bay colonies were not as warm in their ardor for war and independence. Perhaps this is because Americans were fighting against the British for different reasons. The Epilogue also suggests that demographic and economic difficulties faced by Virginia, Maryland, and Massachusetts prior to the American Revolution were not alleviated by that conflict. To what extent do wars alter powerful demographic and economic forces or alter trends?

We usually plan to do a simulation of the trial of Captain Thomas Preston (Chapter 4), so we avoid doing one here. But we have been tempted to have some students assume positions of Virginia Burgesses and others of members of the Massachusetts General Court and discuss/report to the rest of the class. A third group might try to show the "representatives" from Virginia (or Maryland) or Massachusetts the differences and similarities of the problems they face.

For Further Reading

A stimulating early overview that attempts a synthesis of "New Social" historians' research is James A. Henretta, *The Evolution of American Society, 1700–1815: An Interdisciplinary Analysis* (1st ed. 1973).

Good places to begin work on the Chesapeake Bay colonies are Warren Billings, John E. Selby, and Thad W. Tate, *Colonial Virginia, A History* (1988); Aubrey C. Land, *Colonial Maryland, A History* (1981); Lois Carr, et al., eds., *Colonial Chesapeake Society* (1988); Allan Kulikoff, *Tobacco and Slaves: The Development of Southern Cultures in the Chesapeake, 1680–1800* (1986); and Philip D. Morgan, *Slave Counterpoint: Black Culture in the Eighteenth-Century Chesapeake and Low Country* (1998).

An excellent "New Social" history of the Chesapeake is Darrett B. and Anita H. Rutman, *A Place in Time: Middlesex County, Virginia, 1650–1750*(1984). See also their accompanying *Explicatus* (1984).

For demographic and economic changes, see Paul G. E. Clemens, *The Atlantic Economy and Colonial Maryland's Eastern Shore: From Tobacco to Grain* (1980); Robert D. Mitchell, *Commercialism and Frontier: Perspectives on the Early Shenahdoah Valley* (1977); and Edmund Morgan, *American Slavery, American Freedom: The Ordeal of Colonial Virginia* (1975).

There are several excellent studies of New England towns. See especially Philip J. Greven, *Four Generations: Population, Land and Family in Colonial Andover, Massachusetts* (1970); and Robert A. Gross, *The Minutemen and Their World* (1976). For Boston see Gary B. Nash, *The Urban Crucible: Social Change, Political Consciousness, and the Origins of the American Revolution* (1979).

Excellent economic studies of New England include Christine Leigh Heyrman, *Commerce and Culture: The Maritime Communities of Colonial Massachusetts* (1984); Ronald P. Dufour, *Modernization in Colonial Massachusetts 1630–1763* (1987); and James J. McCusker and Russell R. Menard, *The Economy of British America 1607–1789* (1985).

CHAPTER 4

What Really Happened in the Boston Massacre?
The Trial of Captain Thomas Preston

By 1770, Great Britain's power over its North American colonies was extremely vulnerable. Although the protests of a few years before had quieted perceptibly, the mother country's position had deteriorated badly, and Britain's mixture of vacillation and determination had left a residue of confusion, ill will, and the impression that Britain would retreat under pressure. Indeed, the British had backed down after nearly every protest by colonists. On the other hand, two regiments had been sent to Boston to keep order and underline England's determination to enforce its will on the colonies. But those English soldiers entered an environment in which British authority was rapidly dissolving and in which some colonists believed that the soldiers could be pushed around. Moreover, it is now clear that a few Bostonians were willing to create an incident with these soldiers. Hence, although historians generally discount the notion of historical inevitability, all the components for an explosion did exist. In fact, given the combustibility of these components, it would have been difficult to avoid an explosion.

The Problem

For years, numerous history teachers have used variations of this problem; their objectives have been the following.

Content Objectives

1. To understand the events and attitudes that brought about the American Revolution and to assess their comparative importance

2. To examine in some depth one of those events to understand certain dynamics of protest and rebellion

Skills Objectives

1. To be able to construct a probable explanation for an event through analysis of conflicting primary evidence

2. To be able to reconstruct a historical event using incomplete evidence (which is almost always how historians do their work)

3. To be able to build an argument from evidence the same way a lawyer does

This chapter also can be used to stimulate students to think about larger questions, such as the following:

1. What role does the crowd play in history? To what extent does a crowd have a collective mentality and goals? To what extent are people in a crowd manipulated by others in the crowd? Considerable literature exploring these questions is available.

2. Once certain components are mixed together, are the events that result from this mixture close to inevitable? After the 1970 tragedy at Kent State, there was a good deal of debate on this question.

3. Is it possible that the British, rather than being tyrants, were simply unable to control the demographic, economic, and political trends occurring in colonial America, trends that were carrying the American colonies little by little out of the British Empire?

These are not the only larger questions or issues that can be discussed. In fact, most likely you have additional important questions and issues you want to introduce to your students; you can do so by only minimally adjusting the problem.

Background

Events in Boston in 1770 unfolded against a political and economic background of fear, suspicion, and anger. Because students recently analyzed the demographic and economic data from colonial Massachusetts Bay, they should pick up the significance of the "moonlighting" British soldiers without prompting. Again, the death of Christopher Seider is easily recognizable as inflammatory. What may be harder to evaluate is the role of Samuel Adams and his talent for political propaganda. Some students may find viewing the events objectively and accepting the possibility that the soldiers acted in self-defense or were purposely goaded into action particularly difficult, but a good understanding of the many sources of conflict between the community and the soldiers facilitates discussion of the events.

The Method

Some people have used this chapter to demonstrate how several historians (or history students) can examine the same evidence and yet draw dramatically different conclusions. In an important work, *Forms of Intellectual and Ethical Development in the College Years* (1970), William G. Perry, Jr., argues that a typical college classroom generally contains three broad groups of students:

1. Those who believe that every problem has but one answer, which the professor will provide and the students will be required to learn (memorize)

2. Those who believe that every problem has but one answer, but for students to learn, the professor will hide the answer and let the students find it

3. Those who believe that answers are relative and that there can be more than one acceptable answer to any problem

If Perry is correct, instructors face a real obstacle in teaching history. We believe that after a few chapters have been discussed, it is best to confront this obstacle head-on, discussing it with students and trying to point out that several probable explanations of what really happened in the Boston Massacre are possible. Like a real-life jury, students must realize that what the evidence seems to indicate are the most likely, most probable explanations. All three types of Perry's students can accept this premise. Here we often contrast a history problem with one in, say, chemistry. A laboratory experiment in chemistry generally can be reproduced in any other laboratory, now or one hundred years from now. In contrast, we could gather several hundred people on a city street and still not reproduce the Boston Massacre.

In this chapter, you will show students how to become involved with the evidence. Students should ask questions of each piece of testimony as if the witnesses were sitting in class—for example, Where were you standing? What was Preston wearing? Where was he standing?, and so forth.

In addition, we point out that the question of what really happened in the Boston Massacre must be broken down into several smaller questions before a general explanation can be obtained. These questions include, Did Preston give the order to fire? Why did the bells ring? Who rang them?, and so on. Then we send the students out with the evidence.

The Evidence

Except for Captain Preston's deposition, we use selections from testimony given at Preston's trial, taken from *The Legal Papers of John Adams* (vol. 3). We have not modernized spelling, capitalization, or punctuation, so you might have to do some of this yourself (for example, *sentinel* for *Centinel*). We provide definitions of some terms that might give students difficulty [such as *charged bayonets* (Source

4)], include a rudimentary sketch of a musket (Source 5), and include a diagram of the Custom House area (Source 1) in the evidence. Encourage students to use these aids as they examine and analyze the evidence.

Students may find it helpful to divide the witnesses into those who support the prosecution and those who support the defense. If they do so, have them look for consistencies and inconsistencies. Make them keep picking at the evidence, asking questions of it:

1. Why did Captain Preston claim he could not have ordered the soldiers to fire? Is his explanation believable? (Source 2)

2. How does the testimony of Edward Gerrish differ from that of other witnesses about the events leading to the calling of the guard?

3. What important piece of information did Thomas Marshall provide?

4. Who did Ebenezer Hinkley say fired the first shot? Why did he fire?

5. Although Peter Cunningham did not hear Preston give the order to fire, his testimony was considered damaging. How?

6. Is Alexander Cruikshanks's testimony of any value? If so, what is it?

7. Could William Wyatt have been mistaken in his identification of Preston? Do you give great weight to Wyatt's testimony?

8. What parts of John Cole's testimony can be called into serious question?

9. Theodore Bliss spoke of the bells, which were a signal in Boston that a fire had broken out. On hearing the bells, people were supposed to come out of their houses to help fight the fire. How did Bliss explain what happened?

10. Henry Knox injected an interesting—and confusing—problem. What is that problem?

11. Benjamin Burdick said there was an order, but who issued it?

12. Daniel Calef's testimony looks bad for Preston. Are there any problems with it?

13. Robert Goddard's testimony is self-explanatory. What does it add?

14. Diman Morton gives us more information about what Preston wore. Which side does this help?

15. Who ordered the soldiers to fire, according to Nathaniel Fosdick? What does he tell us about Captain Preston?

16. Isaac Pierce's testimony—if true—is particularly damning. Why?

17. How does the testimony of Joseph Belknap support that of Pierce?

18. The testimonies of several people (including Richard Palmes, Matthew Murray, the servant Andrew, Daniel Cornwall, William Sawyer, Jane Whitehouse, and James Woodall) corroborate one another. What do their testimonies add?

19. Is Newton Prince's testimony of any value? What is it?

20. Why is Captain Gifford's testimony important? (If Preston did give an order to fire from charged bayonets, he must have panicked.)

21. What information did Thomas Peck add? How valuable is that information?

22. Which side did Lieutenant Governor Thomas Hutchinson support with his testimony?

Questions to Consider

These questions are fairly self-explanatory. However, some students may ask for more information on the witnesses' backgrounds and attitudes. This is a reasonable request, but such evidence is not available.

We usually have students study the chapter and work with it individually and then meet as a class a few days later to discuss the results. If you like simulations, this is a chapter for one. One former colleague experimented with simulations of other problems (such as the trial of Martin Luther) and informed us that the students got very excited about such exercises. Another colleague assigns two students to prepare the case for the prosecution and two for the defense. Rather than conducting a simulation, these students prepare and represent the strongest cases possible for each side. There is some opportunity for debate and rebuttal. The remainder of the class is the jury. Afterward, the problem is analyzed.

Questions Students Often Ask

After John Adams defended Preston, did Bostonians refuse to hire him as an attorney?

Apparently not. John Adams, however, spent more time in government after 1775 than he did practicing law.

Why was the surtout so important?

The witnesses' ability or inability to state what Preston was wearing that evening was of vital importance because it was a means of determining whether they really did identify him in the confused situation. Remember that it would have been dark in Boston on a March night at 9:00 P.M.

The soldiers testified against their commanding officer. Why? What happened to them?

> If Preston had given no order to fire, the soldiers (whose trials followed that of Preston) would have been in serious trouble, having shot civilians without being ordered to do so. After the trials, the soldiers disappeared from view.

Who was the man (seen by Jane Whitehouse and James Woodall) behind the soldiers?

> We do not know. We know it was not Preston. Students tend to build this individual into a significant figure, assigning him a variety of motives (a Patriot trying to cause trouble; a Tory supporting the soldiers; another British officer, and hence the confusion as to what Preston was wearing).

Is it possible that Preston was guilty?

> It is possible that Preston gave the order but that not all the soldiers heard the order. In that event, he would have panicked (charged bayonets). Often we role-play with students, taking the position that Preston was guilty, to force the arguments.

Epilogue and Evaluation

We do not mention that the three judges virtually instructed the jury to find Preston innocent. After your students complete the problem, you might introduce this point. Although the bulk of the evidence points to Preston's innocence, is it possible that he was guilty after all?

As with the previous chapters, you have considerable leeway in evaluating. Following are a few options:

1. Having students write a brief for either the prosecution or the defense, using all the evidence

2. Conducting a simulation and evaluating the quality of the participants

3. Conducting a discussion, making each student a juror who must explain his or her verdict

A friend of ours collected evidence on the Kent State incident of 1970, distributed it, and asked students to use the same process to evaluate this evidence as they did with the Boston Massacre. This is an interesting exercise, but it may take too much time or be too "presentist" for your taste. Another instructor sets up a debate, based on written prosecution and defense briefs.

For Further Reading

Two good overviews of the American Revolution are Edward Countryman, *The American Revolution* (1985) and, from the British perspective, Colin Bonwick, *The American Revolution* (1991). In *The Cousins' Wars: Religion, Politics, and the Triumph of Anglo-America* (1999), Kevin Phillips emphasizes the commonalities between the English Civil War and the American Revolution. As for the impact of the Revolution, its political language and social message transformed American society, Gordon Wood argues in *The Radicalism of the American Revolution* (1992).

Colonial urban developments are discussed in Carl Bridenbaugh, *Cities in Revolt* (1955); and Gary B. Nash, *The Urban Crucible: Social Change, Political Consciousness, and the Origins of the American Revolution* (1979). Pauline Maier, *From Resistance to Revolution* (1972), surveys public uprisings and civil disorder generally between 1765 and 1776; and Fred Anderson, *A People's Army: Massachusetts Soldiers and Society in the Seven Years' War* (1984) provides insights into the antagonism between the citizens and the soldiers.

Two specific studies on the development of British imperial policies and the American reaction to the implementation of those policies are Joseph Tiedemann, *Reluctant Revolutionaries: New York City and the Road to Independence, 1763–1776* (1997) about the galvanizing effect of the Stamp Act; and Peter D. G. Thomas, *The Townshend Duties Crisis: The Second Phase of the American Revolution, 1767–1773* (1987). The standard study of the so-called Boston Massacre is still Hiller Zobel, *The Boston Massacre* (1970), although some critics have noted that the author tends to be unsympathetic to the crowd and somewhat pro-British.

Fuller studies of some of the major historical actors in this event include two recent biographies of John Adams, John E. Ferling's *John Adams: A Life* (1992); and C. Bradley Thompson's *John Adams and the Spirit of Liberty* (1998). Page Smith, *John Adams,* vol. 1 (1962) offers a good account of Preston's trial from Adams's viewpoint. John C. Miller's classic biography *Sam Adams: Pioneer in Propaganda* (1936) may be supplemented by Pauline Maier's *The Old Revolutionaries: Political Lives in the Age of Samuel Adams* (1980) to gain a sense of the times. Finally, David Hackett Fischer's readable *Paul Revere's Ride* (1994) focuses on his role in the coming of the Revolution, while Jane E. Triber's full biography, *A True Republican: The Life of Paul Revere* (1998) emphasizes his background within the artisan culture, his membership in the Sons of Liberty, and his steadfast republicanism before, during, and after the Revolution.

CHAPTER 5

The First American Party System:
The Philadelphia Congressional Election of 1794

The end of the Revolutionary War left Americans with many unanswered questions. During the century preceding the Revolution, the colonies gradually matured economically and socially, evolving into something quite different from the early settlements. As the colonial statistics (see Chapter 3) demonstrate, population growth, land availability, and migration were altering economic and social patterns and even changing the ways colonists thought and behaved.

Uppermost in American minds, however, were not these patterns (which were barely perceived) but the question of whether a central government could be formed to fulfill the ideals of the Revolution. Although popular and successful in some areas, the Articles of Confederation proved disappointing, especially to propertied groups, those engaged in commercial agriculture, and city dwellers. The 1787 Constitution created a more powerful central government, but one somewhat removed from the people. Partly to bridge this gap and partly from a division over policies, political factions evolved in the early republic. Exasperated, Thomas Jefferson remarked, "If I could not go to heaven but with a party, I would not go there at all." The point, however, was not whether Jefferson would go to heaven with a political organization, but whether he could have gone to the executive mansion without one.

The Problem

Content Objectives

1. To learn about the evolution of the first party system, including early divisive issues, significant events and people, and why federalism ultimately failed

2. To understand the nature of electoral politics in the first party system and the similarities and differences between electoral politics in 1794 and those in our own time

3. To understand how John Swanwick was able to defeat his entrenched opponent, Thomas Fitzsimons

Skills Objectives

1. To understand the major ways elections can be analyzed and to be able to conduct such an analysis

2. To be able to fit together disparate and seemingly unconnected evidence and arrange that evidence to form an explanation for a particular event

3. To be able to use maps in sophisticated ways and to overlay maps on other evidence to discern patterns

On a larger scale, you may want to use the chapter to stimulate thought and discussion on one or more of the following questions or of a wider question or issue that you feel better fits the central themes of your course:

1. What are the functions of political parties in the United States? Why did the founding fathers fear the parties? Have political parties always acted responsibly?

2. Why do voters behave (vote) the way they do? (Recall that a Gallup or Roper poll of approximately sixteen hundred people can usually be used to predict election results with remarkable accuracy.) In other words, are there patterns of voting behavior? What factors (variables) influence that behavior?

3. To what extent do voters make free choices? To what extent are voters manipulated?

4. What are the potential benefits and liabilities of universal suffrage? (Recall that, generally, only white male property owners and taxpayers voted during the early national period.)

Background

Because the American experiment in self-government proved successful, students often view that success as inevitable. They fail to appreciate the fragility of the new republic and the fears of the nation's leaders that Americans would prove incapable of maintaining the virtues considered necessary for self-government.

Could Americans display sufficient intelligence and self-restraint to maintain good order? More importantly, would they elect strong and capable leaders?

Somewhat naively, leaders of the new nation expected to administer the affairs of the nation without factions or parties. Indeed, factionalism was feared as being so potentially divisive as to destroy the republic. However, the problems of the role of the national government, the interpretation of the Constitution, payment of national and state debts, establishment of the Bank of the United States, the encouragement of commerce, and the development of United States foreign policy divided the new representatives to Congress into factions, which gradually coalesced into two opposing parties: the Federalists, under the leadership of Alexander Hamilton, and the Democratic-Republicans, led by James Madison and Thomas Jefferson.

Students must be reminded that, even in Philadelphia, the parties were not well developed in 1794. Characteristics of party politics, such as intensive campaigning and public displays of party support, were not present in the elections of the 1790s. Nevertheless, party affiliation can be surmised from a variety of political and nonpolitical sources.

The Method

In their volume, students are introduced to four principal ways of analyzing elections: studying the candidates, including the images those candidates seek to project; studying the issues and how the candidates respond to those issues (or fail to respond to them); studying the campaigns, including strategy and execution; and studying the voters, using techniques pollsters, campaign strategists, and election analysts pioneered and used.

You must remind students of two important points. First, economic, social, and political institutions change over time. Students often assume that a particular contemporary institution (a church, school, or political party) has always performed the same functions in the same ways. Such a belief makes successful completion of this exercise extremely difficult because political institutions in 1794 were quite different from those today. However, if considerable care is taken, methods used to analyze contemporary elections can be applied to the elections of almost two centuries ago. We point out to students important ways political contests in the 1790s differ from those today. This technique needs some reinforcement if you use it.

Second, we find that many strongly resist the philosophical assumptions that undergird demographic sampling and political polling. The idea that a pollster can predict voter behavior with considerable accuracy by sampling a small (but extremely carefully selected) portion of the electorate strikes some students as offensive, an attack on their uniqueness and individuality. You must overcome this obstacle with great delicacy. When this obstacle does surface (and it has nearly every time we have used this problem), we usually encourage the objectors to state their case as persuasively as they can. Invariably, one or more of the other students will respond, "But if the theory underlying these polls is incorrect, why do they usually work?" At this point, the objectors generally can be brought to a middle ground of accepting uniqueness in some areas and patterns in others. The objective is to establish the point without overly sidetracking the discussion.

Before the students begin tackling the evidence, explain how the evidence is to be arranged. To help students, but without doing their work for them, it is beneficial to introduce the problem using the following two questions:

1. Who voted for each candidate? This answer requires a comparison of election results by ward with occupational breakdown by ward.

2. Why did people vote for a particular candidate? At this point, the four approaches (candidates, issues, campaign, voters) should be reintroduced. Without giving away too much, encourage your students to arrange the evidence to answer these questions. Now they are ready to examine the evidence.

The Evidence

In this chapter, the pieces of evidence are quite disparate, which often worries students. Moreover, the evidence is not arranged in any particular logical order. Hence, in some ways, this exercise is more sophisticated and challenging than those in earlier chapters. More than a little thought and experimentation are necessary for students to understand how the various pieces of evidence relate to one another.

Each student should rearrange the evidence in his or her own way. Here we consider the evidence roughly in the order it is initially presented. Source 1 concerns the candidates. Much of the backgrounds of Thomas Fitzsimons and John Swanwick is similar, a fact that students will be able to pick up. However, there are some differences. Their opposing stands on the excise tax is important and can be linked to Hamilton's and Jefferson's different stances on the Whiskey Rebellion (Sources 4 and 5), the leading newspapers' editorials on the people who supported or opposed the rebellion in western Pennsylvania (Sources 2 and 3), Philadelphia's sugar factories, tobacco factories, and breweries and distilleries (Source 6), and the Democratic Society's position (Source 7)—Swanwick was an officer in the society.[1] Some students also will pick up on Swanwick's aid to immigrants and how that might prove politically beneficial later.

Many students think that religion was a crucial difference between the two contestants. But was it? Fitzsimons had held several previous elective offices. Unless all his opponents had been Roman Catholics (thus canceling out this

---

[1]Students have to rely more strongly on another text in this problem than in previous exercises to get more detailed information on the excise tax, Hamilton and Jefferson, the Whiskey Rebellion, and the Democratic Society.

variable), Fitzsimons must have been supported consistently by the electorate in spite of his religious persuasion.

With a bit of guidance, students will be able to overlay the map of wards (Source 8), the yellow fever epidemic (Sources 12 through 17), the actual vote (Source 18), and the chart showing occupations by ward (Source 9). They should be able to see that although Swanwick attracted votes from all occupations and people with varying degrees of wealth, the bulk of his support came from Philadelphians of more modest occupations and means.

The real problems arise when students confront the cost of living index and the index of real wages (Sources 10 and 11), as well as the data on the 1793 yellow fever epidemic (Sources 12 through 17), which William Powell estimates may have killed as many as 6,000 people, or more than 10 percent of the total population of Philadelphia. Students wonder how these facts relate to the 1794 election. We think that here you can use this disconnected information to establish the attitude of many Philadelphians, especially the nonwealthy. Students may need your guidance to understand the statistical evidence presented in the indices of the cost of living and real wages. Many will be unable to read the charts without an explanation of the concept of the base year. Smith calculated the total costs of food, rent, firewood, and clothing for a workingman in Philadelphia in 1762 at fifty-five pounds. Those costs became the base year for the index (100). Expenditures for other years are read as percentages of the base years. Thus, the cost of food in 1788 was 99 percent of the cost of food in 1762, but by 1789 it had risen to 107 percent of the cost of food in 1762. Similarly, the cost of clothing in 1788 was 139 percent of the cost of clothing in 1762. Similarly, the cost of clothing in 1788 was 139 percent of the cost of clothing in 1762 (or an increase of 39 percent). Once students master the charts (Sources 10 and 11), you can proceed to other questions. Was the overall cost of living increasing or decreasing? Were real wages for laborers rising or falling? What would be the reactions to those phenomena? In 1793, many wealthy people fled the city, closing their businesses and homes and thereby throwing many workers out of jobs. In addition, medical treatment for many of modest means was not readily available, despite Dr. Rush's best efforts. How would people of modest means have reacted to the unavailability of treatment? What effect would Dr. Rush's treatment of the poor have had on their political decisions? And, given what we know of Swanwick, how was he able to profit politically from these feelings? Admittedly, the leap of logic here is a bit far, but with your help, it can be made.

Questions to Consider

The first part of this section in the students' volume helps students link the election results by ward to the chart on occupation by ward. Occupation is used as a proxy for wealth and status, although there are some important exceptions. Merchants, for example, could be found in all but the poorest class. Moreover, doctors in the eighteenth century did not have the status they enjoy today, although many were quite wealthy. These exceptions aside, in general one can see that Swanwick gained most of his strength from wards populated largely by people of moderate means and poorer sorts, especially artisans. Very few laborers were qualified to vote in the 1790s; most artisans in Philadelphia were.

The second part of the section helps students arrange the evidence into the four general approaches (candidates, issues, campaign, voters) and stimulates the students to think about how to connect the evidence in these four general categories. Once students categorize the evidence, they have to bring together the evidence from each category to explain why John Swanwick won the election. What students see when they overlay the evidence is that each general approach points to the same answer: Swanwick won because a large proportion of the middling class (especially artisans) had abandoned Federalism, for various reasons, including the following:

1. Swanwick's attack on the excise tax, a tax that hurt the middling and poorer classes

2. Swanwick's position in the Democratic Society, which appealed to the middling class

3. Swanwick's clever stand on the Whiskey Rebellion, popular with the middling class (especially after Washington denounced the Democratic Society)

4. Inflation, which hurt the middling and poorer classes

5. The yellow fever epidemic, which caused many of the wealthy to flee, leaving the middling and poorer classes unemployed and vulnerable to the fever.

Alternatively, you might emphasize the deterioration of Fitzsimons's popularity because of his unswerving support of Hamilton, who was linked with Philadelphia's aristocracy. Swanwick, although wealthier than Fitzsimons, was able to avoid that image. The key is thus the middling class: how they fared, how they thought and felt, how they behaved.

Questions Students Often Ask

If there were no political parties, who decided who would be a candidate?
Early in the 1790s, friends of the candidates simply offered their names in letters to newspaper editors. There were no printed ballots, so voters could write in whomever they pleased. By 1794, factional leaders met in caucuses and agreed on a ticket.

Why didn't candidates break the unwritten rule and openly campaign for office?
Most voters would have been appalled and would not have chosen such a person. Indeed, not until the late nineteenth century were presidential

candidates extremely active in their own behalfs. A man who coveted an office (Aaron Burr comes to mind) was not to be trusted.

Why did Hamilton push for an excise tax that he knew would be unpopular?
First, the government needed the money. Second, some believe Hamilton actually wanted to provoke an uprising that the government would put down, thus demonstrating the power of the new federal government.

Who would be designated as a "gentleman" (Source 11, chart on occupations by ward)?
A gentleman was a man who owned considerable property and lived on rents. The vast majority of Philadelphia rented their homes and places of business.

What effect did the Genet Affair of 1793 have on this election?
That is very hard to say. It is known, however, that Genet remained popular with Philadelphia artisans even after he was abandoned by the Democratic-Republican faction.

Did Hamilton or Jefferson assist either candidate in the 1794 Philadelphia election?
No. That would have been considered improper because neither was a Philadelphian. Hamilton did help Federalist candidates in New York.

In 1762, Philadelphia workers earned about fifty-nine pounds per year. How much would that be in present dollars?
Historian Billy G. Smith states that Philadelphia workers lived at or near the poverty line, which means that each 1762 pound was worth slightly more than $254 in 1985 dollars (*Federal Register*, March 6, 1986). To help the poor, bread prices were fixed by law in the 1790s, and numerous private charities assisted the "virtuous" poor, people who were judged poor by circumstance, not by indolence.

For Further Reading

There is a rich body of historical literature on party formation both in the new nation and in Pennsylvania. Noble Cunningham, Jr.'s *The Jeffersonian Republicans: The Formation of Party Organization, 1789–1801* (1957) is an excellent overview which has stood the test of time, as has Harry Marlin Tinkcom's *The Republicans and Federalists in Pennsylvania, 1790–1801: A Study in National Stimulus and Local Response* (1950). In *The Whiskey Rebellion: Frontier Epilogue to the American Revolution* (1986), Thomas P. Slaughter explains the threat to the fragile union by the independent "friends of liberty," who sought local autonomy for the frontier against the centralizing influence of the "nationalists." Two helpful recent surveys of factions and party formation are James Roger Sharp, *American Politics in the Early Republic: The New Nation in Crisis* (1993) and John H. Aldrich, *Why Parties? The Origin and Transformation of Political Parties in America* (1995). Stanley Elkins and Eric McKitrick provide a detailed study of the period in *The Age of Federalism: The Early American Republic, 1788–1800* (1993).

For studies of Philadelphia, see Billy G. Smith's *The "Lower Sort": Philadelphia's Laboring People, 1750–1800* (1990), a pathbreaking examination of how the working people of that city fared during the post-Revolutionary era. John K. Alexander's *Render Them Submissive: Responses to Poverty in Philadelphia, 1760–1800* (1980) provides a thorough analysis of the city's socioeconomic classes. Roland M. Baumann's dissertation, "The Democratic-Republicans of Philadelphia: The Origins, 1776–1797" (Pennsylvania State University, 1970) and his subsequent articles in the *Pennsylvania Magazine of History and Biography* provide excellent material on the excise tax, the 1794 election, and Philadelphia politics. *Philadelphia, the Federalist City: A Study of Urban Politics, 1789–1801* (1976) by Richard G. Miller combines quantitative analysis with political narrative. J. H. Powell's *Bring Out Your Dead: The Great Plague of Yellow Fever in Philadelphia in 1793* (1949) is an excellent account of the tragic epidemic that killed nearly ten percent of the city's population.

Historians' growing interest in describing the spread of printing and literacy, analyzing the creation of political culture, and examining parades, fetes, rites, and the uses of symbols has resulted in some exciting new work in the early national period. All three of the following studies include Philadelphia: Simon P. Newman's *Parades and the Politics of the Street: Festive Culture in the Early American Republic* (1997); Len Travers' *Celebrating the Fourth: Independence Day and the Rites of Nationalism in the Early Republic* (1997); and David Waldstreicher's *In the Midst of Perpetual Fetes: The Making of American Nationalism, 1776–1820* (1997). Two articles which focus only on Philadelphia are Lee L. Schreiber, "Sponsors of American Culture: A Social Profile of Philadelphia's Federal Party Activists," *Journal of American Culture* 10 (spring 1987): 79–86; and Albrecht Koschnik, "Political Conflict and Public Contest: Rituals of National Celebration in Philadelphia, 1788–1815," *Pennsylvania Magazine of History and Biography* 108 (July 1994): 209–248.

CHAPTER 6

Land, Growth and Justice:
The Removal of the Cherokees, 1838–1839

Historians of early America generally believe that the most significant accomplishment of Thomas Jefferson's presidency was the Louisiana Purchase of 1803. At once a United States of 888,685 square miles was increased to a nation of over 1.7 million square miles, nearly doubling its size.[1] For President Jefferson, the acquisition of such an enormous amount of land would guarantee that the United States would conform to his dream of a nation of farmers, people who were free because they were landowners.

A darker side of the Louisiana Purchase agreement, however, was that now the United States had acquired land onto which the eastern nations of Native Americans could be relocated. Between the Treaty of Holston (1791), which set the Cherokee boundaries "for all time," and Jefferson's election to the presidency in 1800–1801, public opinion in the Southeast had shifted to a removal policy. Rapid westward expansion after the War for Independence often brought white settlers into Cherokee territory. Thus, in 1802 the U.S. government reached an agreement with the state of Georgia that promised that the government would "extinguish, for the use of Georgia, as early as the same can be peaceably obtained on reasonable terms . . . the Indian titles to all lands lying within the limits of the state."[2]

Thus, as opinion in the Southeast shifted, the Louisiana Purchase lands offered an excellent opportunity for whites to remove eastern Indians from their lands.

---

[1] The actual area of the Louisiana Purchase was not finally determined until the Adams-Onís Treaty of 1819, which set the western boundary of the territory and the 1846 agreement with Great Britain that determined the northern boundary.

[2] Samuel Carter III, *Cherokee Sunset, A Nation Betrayed: A Narrative of Travail and Triumph, Persecution and Exile* (Garden City, N.Y.: Doubleday, 1976), p. 28.

38

The Problem

Content Objectives

1. To learn about the debates in the early nineteenth century concerning the removal of Native Americans to lands west of the Mississippi River

2. To learn about the diverse attitudes that Euro-Americans held toward Native Americans and vice versa

Skills Objectives

1. To be able to analyze the pro and con arguments in a debate

2. To be able to assess the strengths and weaknesses of all positions in a debate

On a larger scale, the whole issue of multiculturalism virtually begs for discussion. To what extent should a racial-cultural minority oppose assimilation into the so-called melting pot? What is gained by such assimilation? What is lost by it? As you can readily imagine, consideration of the evidence in this chapter can elicit extremely warm debate.

Background

This section provides the context for students to understand the debates over the removal of the Cherokees beyond the Mississippi River. It discusses where the Cherokees resided at the time of European contact, the Cherokees's social and political systems, and the Cherokees's increasing dependence on European manu-factured goods. The section then sketches the adaptation of many Cherokees to Euro-Americans' economic, political, and social institutions and practices and ultimately how that adaptation did not save them from efforts to remove them to lands west of the Mississippi River. The section concludes with a short narrative of efforts by Cherokees and their white allies to avoid removal, efforts that in the end were unsuccessful.

The Method

In this section, students are shown how various speakers and writers often *rephrased* the question of why Cherokees should or should not be removed (Jackson, for example, rephrased the question of why the Cherokees could not remain where they were).

As to the second question (the strengths and weaknesses of each argument), students are warned about asking "what-if" questions that ultimately do not tell us much about what actually did happen. For this chapter, those questions can, however, shed light on why things happened. By attempting to get inside the minds of the historical actors, we can perhaps better understand why they acted as they did. But students should take care, and especially *not* attribute twenty-first-century ideas to early nineteenth-century people.

The Evidence

Source 1 is an excerpt from President Jackson's message to the Congress of 1829. Jackson clearly argued that a sovereign state could not be created within an existing state (one need not wonder what he would have thought of South Carolina's December 1860 vote to secede). But Jackson goes on to describe a Native American population facing white encroachment. See the phrase "weakness and decay" as his prophesy of what would happen to Native Americans who remained in the East. Jackson said that this "emigration should be voluntary," but did he really mean that?

Source 2 is an excerpt from President Jefferson's 1808 letter to the Delawares, Mohicans, and Munries. What is Jefferson (who was fascinated with Native American culture) saying to those Native Americans? What is he saying when he writes that "we shall all be Americans; you will mix with us by marriage, your blood will run in our veins, and will spread with us over this great island"? Was Jefferson calling for the biological obliteration of Native Americans? What was his "answer" to the "problem" of Native Americans? Many other figures, including Monroe's secretary of the treasury, William Crawford (an 1824 presidential nominee), proposed intermarriage. Why did that idea not appeal to Native Americans? Students will be able to discuss the extent to which Jefferson's idea for Native Americans was ultimately more destructive than Jackson's removal policy.

Prior to white intrusion, Cherokee women had a considerable voice in public affairs. White missionaries and government agents were shocked and appalled by this relative equality, and busied themselves trying to make Cherokees conform to white ideas about gender relations. Source 3 clearly shows that Cherokee women were not afraid to state their opinions regarding removal. But this 1817 petition demonstrates that Cherokee women who opposed removal were appealing to Cherokee men in what was for them nontraditional ways. The women appealed on behalf of their children and, moreover, viewed men as the chief cultivators of the land. What effects might this appeal have had?

John Ridge (Source 4), a Cherokee leader, offered a somewhat different interpretation of the argument. Ridge seemed to believe that Cherokees could adopt certain ideas and practices of whites and yet merge them into their traditional culture. How could Ridge's "biculturalism" be used to solve Cherokee difficulties? What are the dangers of cultural obliteration?

"William Penn" (Source 5) argued that previous treaties made with the Cherokees guaranteed and protected their land. The writer also argued (incorrectly, as it turned out) that land assigned to the Cherokees was not valuable, and white settlers did not want it. Finally, the writer argued that the notion that whites would invade and pillage Cherokee land and, therefore, the Cherokees should be removed, was specious. If the government wished to protect them, then it could.

Senator Theodore Frelinghuysen (Source 6) strongly disagreed, claiming that Native Americans could live and "flourish in the neighborhood of a white population." He described the Cherokee progress toward "civilization" and countered the notion that proximity to whites was undermining their social and moral fabric.

In all, then, there are five different positions with regard to removal:

1. Remove Cherokees "voluntarily" (Source 1)

2. Biological assimilation (Source 2)

3. Do not remove, but adopt white people's economic practices (Source 3)

4. Do not remove, but mix white and Native American practices (Sources 4 and 6)

5. Do not remove, allowing Cherokees to retain their traditional culture (Source 5)

Publicly no whites advocated the extermination of Native Americans, although Henry Clay and some others came close.

Questions to Consider

In 1969, Fr. Francis Paul Prucha published an article in the *Journal of American History* that raised considerable controversy. One of the leading experts on Native American history, Father Prucha assessed the alternatives available to President Jackson and strongly implied that perhaps removal was the best alternative.[3] This section poses questions to help students clarify their thinking regarding Cherokee removal as well as help them identify the principal arguments of the speakers and writers.

The initial reaction of almost all of our students is to condemn Jackson immediately, without giving him the opportunity to present his case. Even when we remind students that President Jackson insisted that removal of the Cherokees ultimately was the most humane alternative for Native Americans (in that it

---

[3]"Andrew Jackson's Indian Policy: A Reassessment," *The Journal of American History*, vol. 66 (December 1969), pp. 527–539.

would protect them from white intrusion and allow them to preserve their own culture), our students almost line up to rebuke Jackson—and removal. If this is as far as students are willing to go, in the end they will learn almost nothing from this chapter. President Jackson's removal policy might well be legitimately attacked, but *only* after giving it a fair hearing *and* listening to *and evaluating* the other positions (Sources 2 through 6). Therefore, you will have to work very hard to get students to see the *strengths and weaknesses* in *EACH* of the arguments.

Questions Students Often Ask

Why didn't the Cherokees opt for military resistance to their removal?
As seen in the chapter, the Cherokees were badly divided. Also, most were realistic enough to understand that such resistance would be futile and would only serve as an excuse for atrocities.

Do any Native Americans still live east of the Mississippi River?
Around twenty-two nations recognized by the Bureau of Indian Affairs live on reservations east of the Mississippi. The largest group is the Cherokees in North Carolina, approximately twelve thousand. As with all other Native Americans, they have the full rights of American citizenship, plus any special rights accorded them.

How many Native Americans today do not live on reservations?
The 1990 federal census listed approximately 2 million people in the continental United States and Alaska (510 federally recognized tribes). Of that number, roughly 50 percent live on the 278 federal reservations. Most other Native Americans reside in major urban areas (Chicago, Oakland, Los Angeles, Minneapolis, etc.).

Who determines who is a Native American?
Each nation sets its own criteria for membership. In addition, there are numerous groups (126 in 1991) that claim to be Native Americans but are not recognized as such by the Bureau of Indian Affairs (established in 1824). Thus, it is extremely difficult to determine the true number of Native Americans living in the United States.

As you can see, students are not only interested in the history of Native Americans but are also fascinated by contemporary Native American life. In addition to the questions listed above, you are likely to get some about poverty and gambling casinos, religion (most Eastern Band Cherokees are Baptists), and some other subjects.

Epilogue and Evaluation

The Epilogue briefly sketches the history of the Cherokees subsequent to removal. The Cherokee Nation (in Oklahoma) suffered severe diminution of its "promised" lands, alleviated only partially by the discovery of oil on Cherokee land in the twentieth century. As for the Eastern Band, the situation was even more unfortunate, with poverty only partially alleviated by tourism and gambling. Both have been destructive.

In our classes, we have divided students into groups of seven and assigned each one an alternative to be argued in the small group (extermination, biological assimilation, removal, more humane removal, remaining on land and culturally assimilating, remaining on land and retaining traditional culture, remaining on land and mixing white with traditional culture). An eighth student might be tapped as recording secretary to take notes. Midway through the hour, the class reassembles to hear the respective arguments and then discuss them. The discussions have proved to be warm. If there are Native American students in the class, this form of evaluation should be avoided.

For Further Reading

We are fortunate to have so many excellent studies of the Cherokees. Among the best are John R. Finger, *The Eastern Band of Cherokees, 1819–1900* (1984); and *Cherokee Americans: The Eastern Band of Cherokees in the Twentieth Century* (1991); Thomas Mails, *The Cherokee People: The Story of the Cherokees from Earliest Origins to Contemporary Times* (1996); Sarah Hill, *Weaving New Worlds: Southeastern Cherokee Women and Their Basketry* (1997).

On Cherokee removal, the most recent study is Theda Perdue and Michael D. Green, eds., *The Cherokee Removal: A Brief History with Documents* (1995). Also extremely valuable are William L. Anderson, ed., *Cherokee Removal: Before and After* (1991); Duane H. King, ed., *The Cherokee Indian Nation: A Troubled History* (1979); Anthony F. C. Wallace, *The Long, Bitter Trail: Andrew Jackson and the Indians* (1993); F. P. Prucha, "Andrew Jackson's Indian Policy: A Reassessment," *Journal of American History* 66 (December 1969): 527–539; Samuel Carter III, *Cherokee Sunset, A Nation Betrayed: A Narrative of Travail and Triumph, Persecution and Exile* (1976); and Stan Hoig, *Night of the Cruel Moon: Cherokee Removal and the Trail of Tears* (1996). For an interesting analysis of Thomas Jefferson's ideas, see Anthony F. C. Wallace, *Jefferson and the Indians* (1999).

CHAPTER 7

Away from Home: The Working Girls of Lowell

From time to time, particularly during rapid social and economic change, Americans have expressed fears about the disintegration of the family, which often has led to a re-examination of women's roles. The 1920s, 1960s, and 1990s especially illustrate this phenomenon. Americans see the family (and the roles of men and women within that institution) as extremely important because families form the basis of the communities that in turn form the nation. It is within families that basic societal values are passed on, and women, because they have traditionally raised the children, are traditionally responsible for the transmission of these values. Thus any change in the role(s) or "place" of women raises serious questions far beyond those about sex-role stereotypes. In fact, many people fear that such changes may endanger our very society.

In the first half of the nineteenth century, many changes were taking place rapidly. The first political party system was being replaced by new alignments, the westward frontier was expanding, educational standards were rising, and hundreds of women and men were raising questions about American society through reform movements as varied as temperance and abolitionism. Not the least of the changes were those related to economic modernization—development of a transportation network, growth of capital information, urbanization, and the beginnings of the factory system. The need for mill hands seemed a solution to the surplus of young women in New England, but the contemporary view of young women was that they were very different from (and probably better than) men and thus had to be protected and sheltered in the home until they married and began their own families. The Lowell system was an attempt to come to terms with the conflict between the older values and sex-role stereotypes and the newer economic needs. That it failed so completely attests to the difficulties in changing deeply rooted beliefs about women or men.

The Problem

Content Objectives

1. To acquire knowledge about one aspect of modernization—the development of the factory system

2. To understand the dominant nineteenth-century sex-role stereotype, the "cult of true womanhood"

3. To understand why and how the need for factory labor was in conflict with American ideas about the proper place for women

Skills Objectives

1. To become acquainted with prescriptive literature

2. To identify themes underlying this type of primary evidence

3. To infer social fears and anxieties from such evidence

The chapter also raises broader issues that are not fixed in time and space, and you may wish to use the chapter to explore some of these larger questions:

1. How and why are sex-role stereotypes formed? To what degree is there a gap between sex-role stereotypes and the realities of most women's and men's lives?

2. What other means of social control exist in our society today? How do we reward normative behavior? How do we punish deviance?

3. To what degree are homogeneity and conformity important to our own society?

4. Is there any conflict of values involved in the present-day trend of increasing numbers of married women with children working outside the home?

The Method

Generally, students will be able to understand the nature of prescriptive literature; they are familiar with today's prescriptive popular fiction, movies, television series, sermons, and self-help books. Yet students need to be encouraged to think carefully about what the message is, for whom it is intended, who is sending it, and most importantly, why the message is being sent. In setting up this chapter, you may wish to spend some time discussing the establishment of the factory system, the aspect of modernization that made it essential to convince young women to leave the small villages and farms of New England and relocate in the new mill towns and cities. The exercise deals only peripherally with modernization, instead emphasizing the conflict between factory work for young women and the prevalent ideas about the proper place for girls and women. Thus you may want to use part of your lecture to describe the factories themselves, the rapidly changing technology of the textile industry, and the widespread antipathy many Americans felt about urbanization and the development of a European-style working class.

The Evidence

Students will be examining the evidence for a variety of messages. You can easily rearrange the evidence, but it also may be used as it stands to solve the puzzle of why people were so anxious and defensive about Lowell and the factory girls who worked there. Who needed to be reassured? About what kinds of things? In other words, what exactly did Americans fear?

Reverend Henry Mills's account of Lowell in Source 2 is one example of such a reassurance: boardinghouses were clean and homelike, young men and women were housed separately, and there was a 10:00 P.M. curfew. We find students especially sensitive to the regimentation and emphasis on personal morality and proper conduct, regulations enforced by housemothers, overseers, and peers by various means. In fact, students generally react quite negatively to the system and sometimes must be encouraged to put themselves in the place of the factory girls and women to understand why they did not rebel against so many restrictions. Lucy Larcom (Source 13), although advancing the usual argument of dire economic necessity, conveys (almost in spite of herself) a certain resentment toward the limited roles available for sheltered young girls. She also portrays the advantages of working and, finally, holds out the possibility that mill girls could still be "ladies." The *Lowell Offering* (Sources 5 through 12) presented just such a ladylike image to New Englanders (and even to Europeans). Asking students to read through the sample table of contents (Source 5) and describe its tone should clarify this attempt at genteel refinement. Some students may even notice in the contents the two items about old maids, and most will see the editorial statement (Source 6) as clearly defensive.

The conflict between ideas about marriageable "ladies" and wage-earning women living away from home is further clarified in "Dignity of Labor" (Source 7), "Editorial—Home in a Boarding-House" (Source 8), and the angry rejoinder to Orestes Brownson, "Factory Girls" (Source 9). With some guidance, students should be able to reconstruct American anxieties about how young working girls would behave if left on their own and the many ways the girls themselves tried to protect their respectability. "A Familiar Letter" (Source 10) and "Gold Watches" (Source 11) demonstrate the strains (and perhaps mutual jealousy) between more traditional middle-class women and those who worked for wages. Finally, "Song of the Spinners" (Source 12) asserts the kind of moral superiority Americans had traditionally associated with hard work and the ensuing sense of independence they gained.

The pictures of the mill girls (Sources 14 and 15) and the selection of the correspondence between three women and their families (Sources 16 through 21) enable students to examine a few individuals more closely. Leaving home at relatively young ages (sixteen, fifteen, and eighteen), these three women were still tied to their families and wrote home dutifully about their work, church, friends, and boardinghouses. The letters between Delia Page and her foster parents (Sources 20 and 21) illustrate many parents' worst fears: young women away from the watchful eyes of their families and villages falling in with fast company, being seduced by married men, and having both their reputations and their lives ruined.

Questions to Consider

These questions encourage students to move through the evidence systematically, looking for specific responses. However, we think that you will want to recombine these specific answers in a way that will form a broader picture and thus return to the central question: how did people react when the needs of a modernizing economy came into conflict with ideas about women's place in society? In what ways did both the factory owners and the girls who worked in the factories attempt to counteract these anxieties?

Questions Students Often Ask

Was there any connection between urbanization and immigration and the rise of the cult of true womanhood?

There is a strong possibility that the growing perception among the middle class that cities were dangerous places, increasingly populated by "vicious" immigrants, helped develop the feeling that women should be protected and sheltered. Of course, there were other causes as well.

How did middle-class women react to the cult of true womanhood?

Told by "experts" (medical doctors and others) that this was their "natural" place, many women accepted and internalized the concept of true womanhood. Many accepted their role, trading off the limitations imposed for dominion inside the home. Recently, historians have discovered that a number of women did not accept this station. Moreover, because the women at Lowell worked outside their homes, they often were not considered true women. Note *their* reaction to that charge.

If the system was working so well, why did the factory owners tamper with it?

Antiquated machinery and rising costs were cutting into their profits. Increasing production and lowering wages were, the owners felt, their best alternatives.

What finally happened to Lowell?

The shifting of the textile industry to the American South in the late nineteenth and early twentieth centuries left Lowell and other cities in a terrible depressed condition. In the 1980s, however, there was a resurgence in Lowell, as high-technology industries (computers) moved in and revived the area's economy.

Epilogue and Evaluation

By describing the breakdown of the Lowell system—the speedup, the stretch-out, the conversion from company housing to privately owned tenements—the Epilogue foreshadows some of the later grievances of workers attempting to organize. The replacement of native-born New England farm girls and women with immigrant women and children makes it clear that the cult of true womanhood and the idea that the proper place for respectable white middle-class women was in the home would dominate the remainder of the nineteenth century, forming the basis for American Victorianism in the Gilded Age.

There are quite a few ways to evaluate students' understanding of this chapter. If the focus is on prescriptive literature, a panel of students could present contemporary popular literature and analyze the message being conveyed. If you wish to develop writing skills, you can duplicate rules and regulations (perhaps those from a fraternity or sorority pledge booklet) and ask students to write briefly about the message and projected image. Finally, some (or all) of the students can be asked to put themselves in the place of the factory girls, the parents of the girls, and the factory owners and discuss the advantages and disadvantages of the system.

For Further Reading

A good, very brief synthesis of the economic developments of this period may be found in Jacqueline Jones, *A Social History of the Laboring Classes* (1999). Jonathan Prude's study of three New England towns, *The Coming of the Industrial Order: Town and Factory Life in Rural Massachusetts, 1810–1860* (1983) shows the persistence of preindustrial ways alongside industrialization, but his treatment of the "workers" and "operatives" never touches on questions of gender.

The best general overview of working women is Alice Kessler-Harris, *Out of Work: A History of Wage-Earning Women in the U.S.* (1982). Jeanne Boydston's *Home and Work* (1990), a conceptually original discussion of the changes in women's work during this era. Also useful is Susan Porter's edited collection, *Women of the Commonwealth: Work, Family and Social Change in 19th Century Massachusetts* (1996), especially the essay on single women and work in Boston. Teresa Murphy's *Ten Hours' Labor* (1992) analyzes religious, reform, and gender issues in the ten-hour-day movement.

A good starting point for women in the factories is Judith A. Ranta, *Women and Children of the Mills: An Annotated Guide to Nineteenth Century American Textile Factory Literature* (1999). However, historian Thomas Dublin's work must be at the heart of any study of the Lowell girls. The best single account of the day-to-day lives of the factory girls is still *Women at Work: The Transformation of Work and Community in Lowell, Massachusetts, 1826–1860* (1979), which may be supplemented by his edited collection *Farm to Factory: Women's Letters, 1830–1860* (1981). Dublin's study "Women and Outwork in a Nineteenth Century New England Town," in *The Countryside in the Age of Capitalist Transformation: Essays in the Social History of Rural America* (1986), edited by Steven Hahn and Jonathan Prude, points out that the putting-out system coexisted with the factory work for a considerable time in New England. In *Transforming Women's Work: New England Lives in the Industrial Revolution* (1994), Dublin uses quantitative methodology to analyze women shoemakers in Lynn, female garment workers in Boston, and New Hampshire women teachers, as well as Lowell factory girls.

Stephen Mrozowski et al., *Living on the Boott* (1996) employ historical archeology to recreate everyday life between 1835 and the end of the century in the eight boardinghouses belonging to one of the major Lowell mills. The factory girls' resistance to exploitation is examined in Laurie Nisonoff, "Bread and Roses: The Proletarianisation of Women Workers in New England Textile Mills, 1827–1848," *Historical Journal of Massachusetts* (1981): 3–14. Julie Husband, "The 'White Slave of the North': Lowell Mill Women and the Reproduction of 'Free' Labor," *Legacy* 16 (1999): 11–21, also notes the women's resistance to exploitive labor practices and the ambiguities created by women workers in militant roles.

The evaluation of women's "place" during this era must begin with Barbara Welter's classic article, "The Cult of True Womanhood, 1820–1860," *American Quarterly* 18 (1969): 151–174. Mary Beth Norton, "Nineteenth Century America: The Paradox of Women's Sphere," in *Women of America: A History*, edited with Carol Berkin, warns about several pitfalls in the use of prescriptive literature to determine women's place. Christine Stansell, *City of Women: Sex and Class in New York, 1789–1860* (1986) posits that the young, single, working women of New York provided an image that challenged and completed with the cult of domesticity. Although few, if any, historians ever argued that completely separate spheres for men and women actually existed, the recent collection edited by Laura McCall and Donald Yacovne, *A Shared Experience: Men, Women, and the History of Gender* (1998) illustrates many areas of overlapping spheres. Without question, the most helpful summary and careful analysis of the many uses of the concept of "separate spheres" is Linda Kerber's "Separate Spheres, Female Worlds, and Women's Place: the Rhetoric of Women's History," *Journal of American History* 75 (1988): 9–39.

CHAPTER 8

The "Peculiar Institution": Slaves Tell Their Own Story

For approximately one-hundred years, historians debated about slavery in the same terms that northern abolitionists and southern defenders of the system used prior to the Civil War. Was slavery a moral sin that retarded and corrupted southern society? Was the system upheld by mutual love and respect or by force? Was slavery merely an economic necessity that white southerners could not eradicate? Was the institution profitable? Relying almost exclusively on evidence from whites (for example, abolitionist literature, travelers' accounts, and plantation records), historians were only repeating the earlier judgments about whether slavery was good or evil. Early work by certain black historians, notably, Carter Woodson[1], was virtually ignored.

By the 1950s, this debate had become somewhat sterile. During the 1950s, however, African Americans were beginning to ask questions of their own, questions about their present struggle for equal rights, their future in America, their past, and their African heritage. Influenced by this new climate, historians also began asking new questions about slavery. Going beyond the questions of whether slavery was good or evil, historians began examining the nature of slavery itself. One of the most influential—and controversial—historical investigations was Stanley Elkins's *Slavery: A Problem in American Institutional and Intellectual Life* (1959). Borrowing concepts from sociology and psychology, Elkins argued that the slaves had lost their African culture and their will to resist because of the traumatic experiences of being captured and transported to America. Once on the plantation, which Elkins considered a "closed system" similar to that of a prison or concentration camp, the slaves became childlike and dependent and even admired their masters.

---

[1]Woodson was a very prolific historian of black America. Among his many contributions are *The History of the Negro Church*, 2d ed. (Washington, D.C.: Associated Publishers, 1921), *The Mind of the Negro* (New York: Russell and Russell, 1926), with Charles H. Wesley, *The Negro in Our History* (Washington, D.C.: Associated Publishers, 1927), *The Rural Negro* (New York: Russell and Russell, 1930), and *The African Background Outlined* (New York: Negro Universities Press, 1936).

Although many of Elkins's points were later proven erroneous, Elkins played a large part in refocusing the questions historians asked about slavery. Now it became important to know how the *slaves* thought and felt. Were they, as Elkins contended, the products of some kind of prescientific "brainwashing"? Or was what Elkins observed merely a mask, behind which were other thoughts and feelings about themselves, their masters and mistresses, and slavery itself?

The traditional white sources historians used clearly could do little to answer these questions. Historians, borrowing this time from cultural anthropologists and folklorists, thus began discovering that slaves and former slaves had left a bounteous store of evidence: songs, stories, customs, fragments of genealogy, bits and pieces of tradition. Using equal parts care and imagination, historians found that they could reconstruct much of the mind and emotions of men and women once thought to be inarticulate. Of course, now we know that they were far from that.

The Problem

Content Objectives

1. To learn how slaves and former slaves thought and felt about themselves, their masters and mistresses, and ultimately the system of slavery itself

2. To appreciate the complexity of the slave system in the Old South

3. To understand that slaves led complete lives, parts of which whites never saw

Skills Objectives

1. To be able to work with fragments of folklore and oral history to reconstruct the thoughts and feelings of a people who left few written records

2. To sort evidence into subheads or subtopics to answer a larger question

3. To be able to translate indirect testimony (symbols, metaphors, allegories) into thoughts and feelings

On a larger scale, the chapter can stimulate thought and discussion on one or more of the following questions or issues:

1. Is anyone "inarticulate" (in the sense that they leave *no* historical record)? What kinds of evidence—statistical and otherwise—does virtually every person leave?

2. When the evidence so-called inarticulate people left conflicts with traditional historical evidence, what does the historian do?

3. In any society, are there groups who have great difficulty communicating with each other (because they are inarticulate in different ways)? How can those gulfs be bridged?

As in earlier chapters, you may want to discuss other, larger questions or issues. We form such larger questions in our lectures introducing the topic.

The Method

We generally use an introductory lecture(s) to introduce the topic of slavery in the United States, usually emphasizing its origins, evolution, increasing rigidity, and principal characteristics. We purposely omit the slaves' perspectives, suggesting only that the slaves may have had a different view and that discovering that view will be the students' task.

We also find it helpful to talk briefly about folklore and oral history and their value as historical tools. We choose a contemporary song familiar to students and work with them to find that song's message. We ask students why people often take the shapes of animals in stories. Does the story form make the message bearable? Why might it be too painful otherwise? You may want to help students see these points before turning them loose with the evidence.

Once students are attuned to picking up hidden messages, their next obstacle is arranging the evidence. In the students' text, we suggest that they can break the central question down into subquestions (for example, how did slaves feel toward their masters and mistresses?) and then marshal all the evidence directly relating to those subquestions. This is not a difficult technique, but you will probably have to reinforce this suggestion.

As usual, we urge students to jot down notes as they go along. One helpful format is:

Subquestion: How did slaves feel about _____?

Piece of evidence   *Brief description of evidence*   *Message*

Other formats can be just as effective.

The Evidence

The evidence is divided into three sections: reminiscences of former slaves (interviewed in the 1930s) (Sources 1 through 16), songs (Sources 17 and 19 through 23), and two narratives of escaped slaves (Sources 24 and 25). The reminiscences clearly show the slaves' mental independence, which the masters and mistresses may not have observed. Indeed, there often is barely concealed hostility toward masters and mistresses. At the same time, one can detect a self-deprecating tone. This is a curious mixture, and a very human and humane one.

You might ask students whom the animals represent (stand for) in stories in which animals are used as representations. Could killing the parrot (Source 2) have been a proxy for killing the mistress? The story of the tortoise is another good example (Source 5), but note how the tortoise story here differs significantly from the "traditional" story of the tortoise and the hare. Why? The traditional story emphasizes that success comes through diligence and hard, steady work. Could slaves have agreed with that moral? The alternative ending speaks much more directly to the slaves' experiences.

Religion comes up again and again. Yet is seems clear that these fragments of evidence are not intended to be taken as remembrances about religion.

The songs were selected to show various emotions: frustration, anger, humor, hope, even latent violence. They can be handled with some ease because their messages often are not so subtle.

The narratives of Frederick Douglass and Harriet Jacobs were intended to further abolitionist sentiment in the North, yet they reveal a good deal about how some slaves rebelled against slavery and, at great personal risk, escaped to the North. Both writers describe real incidents from their own lives, and both differentiate between "good" and "bad" whites while rejecting the institution of slavery completely. Students will readily recognize Douglass's burning desire for education and the sense of personal self-worth that enabled him to fight back against the "slave-breaker." Jacobs, an attractive young slave woman, also was vulnerable to sexual exploitation, not only by her own master but also by Mr. Sands. Jacobs's narrative also sheds light on the complex relationships between black and white women and between black women and their families.

Finally, putting together all the answers to the subquestions, students should find it evident that slaves themselves had an interesting mixture of thoughts and feelings about the "peculiar institution." You might ask your students to think about why slaves hid those thoughts and feelings from whites. What would slaves show to whites in place of those thoughts and feelings?

Questions to Consider

In this section, students are encouraged to devise a number of subquestions (we provide four possibilities). Then together we pare down their suggestions to a manageable number. You also might remind your students that several pieces of evidence may fit more than one subquestion.

Once the students reassemble in class, we begin addressing the subquestions one by one. Occasionally, a piece of evidence needs to be extracted and examined in some depth. As much as we can, we try to get the students to do this process themselves, from time to time asking a question to get things moving. Finally, we get students to put all the evidence together, answering the central question.

You may have to exert special effort to teach your students to express themselves more articulately. For example, one of our students offered the thesis that "slaves thought slavery was bad." The answer was OK, but it was a disappointing, shallow thesis that could have been offered without the benefit of taking the course at all. "What *specifically* did they think was bad about it?" is our usual response to such an offering. In other words, we try to push the students back into the evidence. Most students respond very well. After all, they have put in a good deal of work and want to get something out of it.

Questions Students Often Ask

Were white people so ignorant that they failed to understand the double meanings of the slaves' songs and stories?

No, but whites were used to thinking of slaves as a simple, docile, childlike people and hence usually missed or overlooked these semihidden messages. Also, many of these songs and stories were sung or told when whites were not around. See the introduction to Gilbert Osofsky's *Puttin' on Ole Massa* (1969).

How can we tell whether the events former slaves depicted in their reminiscences actually took place?

We cannot tell with absolute certainty whether these events occurred. According to Osofsky, "The most obviously false accounts readily give themselves away." Moreover, even if many of these events did not actually take place, the reminiscences still provide clues to what slaves *wanted* to take place.

Were the former slaves who were interviewed in the 1930s a representative sample?

No, they were not. A greater proportion of people interviewed had been slaves in the lower South, the "cotton South." Also, fewer than 20 percent of those interviewed had been more than twenty years old in 1865. Most had been slave children, freed before reaching adulthood. Most adult slaves had died by 1930: the average life expectancy of a slave in 1850 was less than fifty years.

Did any of the people interviewed look back on their lives as slaves more fondly?

Yes, a small number did. Because many of the interviewers were white, however, some of these reminiscences may have been purposely distorted. Why would a black person in the 1930s purposely have been less than candid?

ʾ ᵗilogue and Evaluation

ʾlogue is a bit different from those in other chapters. Rather than placing
ᵐm in its historical context (a very difficult undertaking), the Epilogue

reinforces the earlier contention that slaves, former slaves, and their descendants possess a rich oral tradition, fragments of which are still being passed down.

There are numerous options for evaluation. Following are four that we recommend; undoubtedly you already have other ideas.

1. Give students additional material (see For Further Reading) and require that they write an essay on how that additional material supports or alters their original thesis on what slaves thought and felt about the peculiar institution.

2. Assign students additional material but have them report orally, either collectively or individually.

3. Evaluate the discussion of the exercise.

4. Select stories, nursery rhymes, or bedtime stories Americans use today and instruct students to delve into their meanings, either in writing or orally.

For Further Reading

There is a vast literature on almost every aspect of slavery in the United States from the seventeenth to the mid-nineteenth centuries. For a short survey, see Peter Kolchin, *American Slavery* (1993); a more detailed account may be found in Ira Berlin's *Many Thousands Gone: The First Two Centuries of Slavery in America* (1998). Three classic analyses of slavery include George Rawick, *From Sundown to Sunup* (1972); Eugene D. Genovese, *Roll, Jordan, Roll: The World that Slaves Made* (1974); and John W. Blassingame, *The Slave Community* (rev. ed. 1979). Vincent Harding, *There Is a River* (1981), offers an interpretation from an African American point of view of the pre-1865 struggle for freedom and justice.

For a fascinating look at the interrelationships among slave traders, buyers, and slaves themselves, see the recent prize-winning study by Walter Johnson, *Soul by Soul: Life Inside the Antebellum Slave Market* (1999). A good introduction to slave culture is Lawrence Levine, *Black Culture and Black Consciousness: Afro-American Folk Thought from Slavery to Freedom* (1977). Sterling Stuckey, "Through the Prism of Folklore: The Black Ethos in Slavery," *Massachusetts Review*, vol. 9 (1968), pp. 417–437, Dana Epstein, *Sinful Tunes and Spirituals* (1977), and John Michael Spencer, *Black Hymnody* (1992) all analyze music and its place in African American culture. On slave Christianity, see Albert J. Raboteau, *Slave Religion: The "Invisible Institution" in the Antebellum South* (1978); on kinship relations, see Herbert G. Gutman, *The Black Family in Slavery and Freedom, 1750–1925* (1976).

This chapter utilizes only a very small number of the slave narratives. Additional selections from the 1930s Federal Writers project may be found in B. A. Botkin, ed., *Lay My Burden Down: A Folk History of Slavery* (1945) and Gilbert Osofsky, *Puttin' on Ole Massa: The Slave Narrative of Henry Bibb, William*

Wells Brown, and Solomon Northup (1969). A recent collection published in cooperation with the Library of Congress is Ira Berlin et al., eds., *Remembering Slavery*; this work also includes two cassette tapes of slave narratives, some from original recordings and others read by well-known actors and actresses. The literary form and place of the narratives are subjects of Paul D. Escott, *Slavery Remembered: A Record of Twentieth Century Slave Narratives* (1979) and Charles T. Davis and Henry Louis Gates, Jr., eds., *The Slave's Narrative* (1985). Two additional collections of primary documents are Willie Lee Rose, ed., *A Documentary History of Slavery in North America*, and John W. Blassingame, ed., *Two Centuries of Letters, Speeches, Interviews, and Autobiographies* (1977).

In this chapter, the examples of runaway slaves came from Harriet A. Jacobs, *Incidents in the Life of a Slave Girl, Written by Herself*, edited by Jean Fagan Yellin (1987) and Frederick Douglass, *Narrative of the Life of Frederick Douglass* (1963). These may be supplemented by John Hope Franklin and Loren Schweninger, *Runaway Slaves: Rebels on the Plantation* (1999), which includes contemporary material such as newspaper reports and county court records. A literary analysis of this literature may be found in Sterling L. Bland, Jr., *Voices of the Fugitives: Runaway Slave Stories and Their Fictions of Self-Creation* (2000).

CHAPTER 9

Slavery and Territorial Expansion:
The Wilmot Proviso Debate, February 1847

Almost all college students come to the study of the Civil War and the trends and events leading up to that terrible conflict with preconceived ideas. Some have developed their ideas from films such as *Gone with the Wind,* or from television documentaries such as Ken Burns's public television series, or even from reading contemporary debates such as those about the symbolism of the Confederate battle flag. And yet, from whatever perspective students approach that part of the American past, almost all will concede that the institution of slavery played an important role in the coming of the Civil War.

It is not clear to many students, however, what *precisely* it was about slavery that helped to bring on that conflict. This chapter suggests to students two important phenomena: (1) the conflict between northern and southern whites was less over whether slavery should *exist* but rather whether it should be allowed to *grow* in the territories (hence a debate over America's *future*), and (2) by the mid-1840s northern and southern whites were beginning to disagree sharply over the intentions of the founding fathers and constitutional rights (hence a simultaneous debate over America's *past*). Perhaps an understanding of these two phenomena will help students to appreciate why intersectional compromises were increasingly unlikely, and ultimately doomed to failure.

The Problem

Content Objectives

1. To understand the major points made by both pro-proviso and anti-proviso speakers

2. To understand the points of disagreement among *northern* debaters and not just the divisions between North and South

3. To analyze why sectional differences seemed less likely to be smoothed over by compromises . . . as had been the case in the past

Skills Objectives

1. To become acquainted with the basic methods of rhetorical analysis

2. To be able to judge the extent to which the rhetoric in the House of Representatives showed an erosion or breakdown of unifying principles or ideas that held the nation together

To paraphrase Edmund Burke, when people begin to define their *rights*, you have a sure symptom of an ill-conducted state. Students need to understand why issues that could be settled by compromise in 1787 or 1820 could not be so easily dealt with by the 1840s. Students should ask to what extent the debate was shifting to *moral* positions (harder to compromise) *or* why political and economic questions that previously had been put off could less easily be deferred.

Background

This section develops the context in which the debate over the Wilmot Proviso of February 1847 can be analyzed. The major thrust here is to link the important force of westward expansion with the institution of slavery. Should slavery be allowed to "follow the flag"? How might people in different sections of the United States define the powerful term *Manifest Destiny*? At the same time, the Background section sketches the intrusion of the slavery question into several American institutions (religious denominations, the right to petition Congress, the privacy of the United States mail, and so forth). Indeed, even those men and women who did not own slaves, lived far from anyone who did, and were not directly affected by the institution found that they could not escape the growing debate over the "peculiar institution."

The Method

Students should not have any trouble identifying the major points made by both the proponents and opponents of the Wilmot Proviso (they have done this already for Chapter 6, on Cherokee removal). Answering the other two questions on how fundamental the disagreements were and how likely these differences were ⌐ nable to compromise, however, will not prove so easy. As noted above, issues vhich there are fundamental differences of moral or ethical opinions are ɔre difficult to settle by means of give-and-take or compromise. What your ·ill need from you is an explanation of why what once were differences of

opinion over economic or political issues by the mid-1840s also had become opposing moral positions as well. Were California and the Northwest Territory the
"last chances" for slaveholders to expand their economic/labor system or for free
farmers to insure their own futures? Or had something changed between 1820 and
1847 that made the issue of slavery expansion impervious to compromise?

The Evidence

Students almost immediately recognize that all but two of the fourteen congressmen whose speeches were excerpted for the Evidence section were Democrats. Thus
students understand that, in addition to the critical issue of the expansion of
slavery, the fierce debate also was over control of the Democratic party. As
explained in earlier sections of the chapter, many northern Democrats were
angered by what they considered to be President Polk's pro-southern stands on the
tariff, internal improvements, the independent treasury, and the settlement of the
Oregon boundary question. Wilmot also may have been embarrassed and angered
by Polk's ignoring of the Pennsylvania congressman's patronage recommendations.
Students, therefore, cannot completely ignore the political in-fighting in the
Democratic party that surfaced in the debate over the Wilmot Proviso (see especially Sources 4 and 5).

A more important political question, however, was the growing sectional
dispute over the control of the federal government. It is possible that this issue
sometimes was cloaked in the guise of the constitutionality of the proviso (see
Sources 2, 7, 8, and 9 especially), but often the issue of which section would dominate the federal government came to the surface (Sources 6, 7, 10, and 11 especially).

John Pettit's speech (Source 1) was included in the Evidence, even though it
technically was delivered before the commencement of the Wilmot Proviso
debate. It was included because Pettit raised the issue of disunion, which Pettit
himself opposed. Although R. W. Roberts denied that southerners were disunion-
ists (Source 2), the spectre of the breakup of the Union appears to have hovered
over much of the debate (breaking to the surface most dramatically in Sources 1, 2,
3, and 14). But several congressmen recognized the profoundly different economic
systems of North and South (see especially Sources 2, 3, 6, and 13).

A number of northern congressmen maintained that the northern states had
given in to the South many times in the past and that the days of compromise
were over (Sources 3, 7, 9, 10, and 13 especially). Richard Brodhead (Source 8)
offered the interesting argument that California *already was* free territory and
that the proviso, therefore, was not necessary. He claimed that Congress would
have to *make* the territory a slave territory. But Howell Cobb (Source 6) earlier
maintained that slavery and compromise had been linked since the beginning of
the republic, and that this would have to continue if the two sections were to
retain political parity.

Several sources appear to show, however, that the chances of compromise were rapidly eroding. Threats of disunion, of course, are one clue. But so is the wrangling over biblical interpretation (Joshua Giddings, in Source 14, said he would rather be a heathen than worship a god that approved of slavery). Even Wilmot himself, who stated firmly that he was no abolitionist, said that the time for compromise was over. And Paul Dillingham (Source 13) said that California should remain free as a haven for *southern nonslaveholding whites.*

Questions to Consider

This section encourages students to cluster the fourteen speeches around four central points:

1. constitutionality of slave expansion

2. politics of the proviso

3. biblical differences

4. slavery and westward expansion

In addition, it points students toward one section's criticism of the other's economic system (especially Roberts's attack on the wage slavery of the northern states, in Source 2) and the threats to the Union.

Questions Students Often Ask

Did the rival Whig party gain from Democratic party divisions?
>   Ultimately not. It is true that in 1848 General Zachary Taylor, the Whig candidate for president, won the election with 47.4 percent of the popular vote over Democrat Lewis Cass (42.5 percent) and Free-Soiler and former President Martin Van Buren (10.1 percent). Many of Van Buren's votes came from disaffected northern Democrats (like Wilmot himself). Yet the Whig triumph was short-lived and the Democrats recaptured the presidency in 1852 (Franklin Pierce won 50.9 percent of the popular vote and 254 of the 296 electoral votes) and the Whig party split into sections and collapsed. Most northern Whigs joined the new Republican party.

How can we say that compromise was increasingly difficult when there actually was a compromise in 1850?
>   It is true that there was a compromise in 1850. But it was a compromise that could not hold. The new Fugitive Slave Act was, according to historian Ronald Walters, "the most provoking of all political events" (see *The Antislavery Appeal* [1976], p. 29). By allowing the vigorous pursuit, recapture,

and return of runaway slaves, the law led to outbreaks of violence and increasing determination by many whites in the North to disobey the law. By the time of the Dred Scott decision, the Compromise of 1850 was in effect dead.

Was David Wilmot politically ambitious?
Yes, but he was also somewhat lazy, relying on his oratorical talents rather than hard work.

Why did Congress go to the trouble of introducing and passing the Wilmot Proviso as late as 1862?
Remember that President Abraham Lincoln maintained that the war was to restore the Union, not to abolish slavery. Indeed, his preliminary Emancipation Proclamation of September 1862 guaranteed that those states that rejoined the Union prior to January 1, 1863 would be permitted to retain the institution of slavery. So the expansion of slavery technically was still an issue on June 19, 1862 when the proviso was passed.

Epilogue and Evaluation

It became increasingly clear as the debate over the Wilmot Proviso unfolded that northerners and southerners alike understood that the future of the West determined the future of the republic. As noted in the Epilogue section, Congressman Preston King stated most clearly the opinion of an increasing number of northern whites when he warned that if "slavery is not excluded [from the territories] by law, the presence of the slave will exclude the laboring white man." As for the South, Howell Cobb of Georgia articulated the fear that blocking the westward expansion of slavery "would be to draw around the southern portion of the United States a cordon of free States, where they 'would light up the fires of liberty. . . .'" With such different views of the West's future and with the West appearing so critical to each section, one can see why compromise was so difficult, if not completely impossible.

In our view, understanding the nature of the 1847 debate over the Wilmot Proviso is so critical to an understanding of the events of the next decade and the nation's descent into disunion and an awful war that we require students to write a one-page or two-page essay that answers the question of whether or not compromise was possible. Each of the major points raised by the respective debaters that will help to answer that question must be included in the essay. In class, we ask a few students to read their essays in order to open up a general discussion on the subject.

For Further Reading

Excellent overviews are Michael A. Morrison, *Slavery and the American West: The Eclipse of Manifest Destiny and the Coming of the Civil War* (1997); Anders Stephenson, *Manifest Destiny: American Expansion and the Empire of Right* (1995); David Potter, *The Impending Crisis* (1976).

On the Wilmot Proviso, see Don E. Fehrenbacher, *The South and Three Sectional Crises* (1980); Chaplain W. Morrison, *Democratic Politics and Sectionalism: The Wilmot Proviso Controversy* (1967); Paul H. Bergeron, *The Presidency of James K. Polk* (1987); Charles Buxton Going, *David Wilmot, Free Soiler* (1924); Thomas M. Leonard, *James K. Polk: A Clear and Unquestionable Destiny* (2001); Joel H. Sibley, *The Shrine of Party: Congressional Voting Behavior, 1841–1852* (1967).

CHAPTER 10

The Price for Victory: The Decision to Use African American Troops

The events surrounding the American Civil War are among the most scrutinized in United States history. Both professional scholars and nearly obsessed amateur historians have studied almost every military engagement with the utmost precision. The results have been thousands of books and articles, numerous annual reenactments, and almost countless local societies devoted to even more intense examinations and analyses of that bloody conflict.

Nearly every amateur historian and many professionals consider the American Civil War essentially a war fought by white men and boys. African Americans appearing in the story are more often treated as passive objects, people over whom the war was fought but who took little active interest in the conflict. This chapter only partially alters that perception, in the Epilogue section, where African Americans' service in the Union army and navy is briefly sketched. The chapter does, however, make it clear that northern blacks were willing and eager to be more than passive objects but were prevented from being so by the timidity of northern white political leaders. Hence the chapter also introduces the issue of northern racism in the Civil War. On the southern side, the tension between ideals and survival, a tension often noted by historians, is highlighted in the Confederacy's tortuous path to the use of African America troops.

The Problem

Content Objectives

1. To understand the shifting war aims in the North and the reasons for those alterations

2. To understand the tension in the South between idealism and survival

3. To understand the extent to which racial prejudice was a problem in the United States during the Civil War

4. To understand efforts of northern blacks to participate in the Civil War and why the aid of blacks was not immediately sought

5. To understand the political and diplomatic problems that President Lincoln faced

6. To understand the divisions in both the North and the South over war aims and arming African Americans

Skills Objectives

1. To be able to follow and analyze a *changing* argument (up to now, students have not had to follow an argument through time)

2. To be able to compare principal arguments in two different sections of the nation over the same issue

3. To be able to recognize that a piece of evidence can be used in a number of ways, depending on the questions that are asked of it

4. To be able to combine historical evidence, logic, and historical imagination to solve a historical problem

On a larger scale, you may want to use the chapter to stimulate thought and discussion of one or more of the following topics:

1. To what extent was racial prejudice the real problem that the Civil War did not address? To what extent does that problem still remain?

2. Could the South have armed the slaves and still kept their original war aims intact? Would arming slaves have made a significant difference in the war's outcome?

3. To what extent are ideas the products of pragmatic necessity? In other words, what external factors influence the creation of ideas?

Background

With their knowledge of the heated debates over slavery that led up to the Civil War, students may be surprised by both sides' reluctance to declare the preservation or abolition of slavery as a war aim. You may have to remind students of the racial attitudes of the North and South, the importance of the slaveholding border states to the Union war effort, and the strategic vulnerability of Washington, D.C. Besides understanding the two sides' rationales for the war, students must be made aware of the changes in attitude on both sides as the war progressed. In both the North and the South, mounting costs and rising casualty lists produced public pressure to end the war as quickly as possible, and many came to view the use of African American troops as a necessity.

This chapter has the luxury of having the greatest amount of setup time; we usually follow our discussion of the Mexican War with classes detailing the events leading up to Fort Sumter. During these classes, we introduce the issues and considerations this chapter covers, such as the rise of the southern fire-eaters, increasing northern intransigence, intrusion of the slavery issue into American lives and institutions, northern white racism, political and constitutional debates over slavery and its extension, and the failure of earlier compromises.

The Method

Ways of approaching the American Civil War are as varied as the number of people who teach it. The core question is what the Civil War was. To some people, it was a struggle between evolving industrial capitalism and agriculture, or between states' rights and a federal system. Others see it primarily as a conflict over the westward expansion of slavery. Still others compare the American Civil War to the movements for national consolidation elsewhere in the Western and non-Western world [see the treatment of the Civil War by R. R. Palmer and Joel Colton in *A History of the Modern World* (6th ed. 1983)].The list of interpretations is nearly endless.

The fact that the American Civil War was very likely all these things and more does not help us much. Even so, we believe that the decisions in the North and South to use African Americans as soldiers can be analyzed in the context of all of these interpretations because those decisions involved complicated constitutional, political, military, diplomatic, and attitudinal questions. Indeed, the chapter can be used to point out how these questions and issues interconnect.

By now, most of our students are able to work their way through an argument, summarizing and taking notes to be used in later class discussions. They also are able to use their intuition to find hidden arguments and material between the lines. In one sense, then, this chapter is partly a review of earlier skills, a sharpening of those skills, and practice in the use of the skills with somewhat more complicated material (in which arguments change over time). The chapter also requires students to use their historical imaginations to describe the implications of the decisions in both the North and the South to use African American troops.

The Evidence

First, students must carefully read through the evidence, listing pro and con positions in both the North and the South on the arming of African Americans. Students have done this in earlier classes and should have little trouble. You will have to point out, however, that some of the evidence for the North does not deal specifically with this question because it only *implies* why Lincoln changed his mind, and on the surface it makes no argument either for or against arming African Americans. See, for example, Source 4, "Lincoln's Proclamation Revoking General Hunter's Order of Military Emancipation," the diaries and notes of Salmon P. Chase (Sources 5, 6, and 8) and Lincoln's letters to Hannibal Hamlin and Carl Schurz (Sources 13 and 14). The *New York Times* editorial (Source 20) does not help much here. These pieces, however, will be used later.

On the southern side, the principal arguments for and against the arming of African Americans, although a bit more complicated, are similarly easy to extract. The complications arise over the issue of whether African Americans who would fight for the Confederacy should be rewarded with their freedom. Indeed, arguments over that issue call into question President Davis's assertion that the war was principally for southern independence [see especially the *Richmond Enquirer* letter, November 4, 1864 (Source 29)].

Now students are ready to compare the pro and con arguments of the North and South. The similarities should be striking to your students, especially the pragmatic argument that soldiers were needed [as, for example, in Frederick Douglass's editorial for the North (Source 3) and General Cleburne's letter for the South (Source 24)] and the opposition arguments that the African Americans would not fight and that whites would not fight side by side with blacks [*New York Tribune* for the North (Source 10) and several letters to editors for the South (Sources 23 and 32)]. The principal differences between the North's and the South's arguments concern the issue previously mentioned of the South's freeing slaves who would fight for the Confederacy [see especially the *Richmond Enquirer* letter of November 4, 1864 (Source 29), Howell Cobb's speech (Source 30), and the *Lynchburg Republican* article of November 2, 1864 (Source 32)].

The similarities between the two sides' views almost invariably lead students to question the racial opinions in the North and South. But to say that both northern and southern whites were racially prejudiced is not enough; many students knew that *before* they enrolled in any history courses. The reminiscences of black and white soldiers in the Union army reveal the racial prejudices African Americans experienced (Sources 2, 11, 16, 17, and 19). The *Richmond Enquirer* letter of November 4, 1864, reveals an even more malicious image of African Americans as people who would turn on their masters. Try to get students to be as specific as they can be when describing the northern and southern white images of blacks. In this light, how is one to interpret the *New York Times* March 7, 1864, editorial (Source 20)?

The factors leading to policy changes are best seen by having students retrace the evidence, using Lincoln's letters to Hamlin and Schurz. Clearly, both Lincoln and Davis resisted the use of African American soldiers, hoping that the war could be won without them. But both men were driven to change their positions by desperation—in Lincoln's case, by problems of filling the ranks and the erosion of his political position.

Finally, students must use logic and their historical imaginations to assess the military, social, and ideological implications of the ultimate decisions to use African American troops. The military implications are the easiest to assess (see the Epilogue in the student text). One question to use to stimulate thought on the other implications is whether the decision in either the North or the South denoted a shifting racial attitude of whites toward blacks. Is there any proof that any such shift took place? As you realize, although your students may not, almost all the evidence points to a negative answer.

Some interesting side questions include the following:

1. How would northern whites have replied to Frederick Douglass?

2. Do President Lincoln's remarks on August 4, 1862 (Source 9), and September 13, 1862 (Source 12), imply that he was beginning to soften?

3. The *New York Times* editorial (March 7, 1864) speaks of a "prodigious revolution" in northern white opinion. Was this an accurate statement?

4. Why was Cleburne silenced?

5. In the *Lynchburg Republican* article (November 1864) (Source 32), the notion of whites as the "master race" was separated from the issue of slavery. How was this opinion a harbinger of the future?

6. The woman who wrote to the *Macon Telegraph and Confederate* (January 11, 1865) (Source 34) pitches her arguments on an almost totally emotional plane. How effective is this?

7. Section 5 of the act of the Confederate Congress of March 13, 1865 (Source 36), is of particular interest. Why was this section included in the act?

Questions to Consider

In this section, we show students the following:

1. Whenever a new question is asked, the student must re-examine evidence with that question in mind.

2. What a piece of evidence will tell a student depends on the question the student asks of it.

3. To assess the implications of a decision, logic, historical imagination, and more evidence are needed. The logic and imagination are used to devise working hypotheses; the additional evidence is used to prove the hypotheses.

The third point is one that students may find difficult without your help. Up to now, they have been *given* evidence and asked to summarize, hypothesize, analyze, and rearrange. But they have never been asked to *go search for evidence*. By now, however, they should have a relatively good idea of where such evidence might be: testimonies in hearings, statistics, reports of incidents, presidential messages, election campaign material, diaries, folklore, and so forth. An excellent review of the entire course is to make students think about where additional evidence might be located. In this way, they will see the whole course coming together.

Questions Students Often Ask

Why were many northern blacks so anxious to fight for a government that discriminated against them?

One important motive was ideological: to put an end to slavery under which so many of their fellow blacks labored. In addition, many African Americans believed that if they proved themselves worthy in battle, they would eradicate much of the racism that existed in the North. Many African Americans served in World War I and World War II for the same reason.

Were there northern leaders who advocated enlisting African Americans prior to Lincoln's decision to do so?

Yes, there were a number of such people. An important one was Gideon Welles, Lincoln's secretary of the navy, who favored that policy and supported equal pay for African American volunteers.

Why were African American casualties so high?

African American troops were often used in very difficult and high-risk situations. In addition, their white officers usually were not of the best caliber, were often incompetent, and were occasionally intoxicated, as was evident in the Battle of the Crater, 1864.

Did Confederates ever capture black Union soldiers? If so, what did they do to them.

Confederates did take black prisoners. These prisoners were treated harshly, as an example to other African Americans, and were often executed.

Did any African Americans ever participate as soldiers on the Confederate side?

As far as we can tell, no black units ever did so. However, there were persistent rumors, which historians have been unable to corroborate, that some individuals did fight in some battles on the southern side. There is considerable misinformation on this question on some web sites.

Epilogue and Evaluation

As noted above, the Epilogue completes the story, showing the North's use of African American troops and the Confederacy's nonuse. From time to time, old stories about a black Confederate soldier or fighting unit here or there (we heard recently of a black soldier who participated in the Confederate assault on Knoxville, Tennessee, in November 1863) have been reviewed, but to our knowledge, no documented evidence proves that African Americans served the Confederacy as soldiers. The Epilogue also reintroduces the question of racism, one that regrettably has outlasted slavery.

For most instructors, this chapter comes at or near the end of the course, so most prefer not to evaluate this problem in writing but to conduct a discussion and evaluate its level and individual contributions. Some of our colleagues assign students roles (for example, northern blacks, or northern whites in favor of arming blacks) to play and present their cases in debate-like fashion. This effectively focuses attention on the major points, and students study the evidence more rigorously if they know they must present a "case."

We occasionally ask our students to write a newspaper editorial for a northern or southern newspaper taking a stand on arming African Americans, supporting that stand with evidence, and dealing with potential arguments against their position. This exercise works well, and most students do a very good job.

For Further Reading

The best general study of the Civil War era is still James M. McPherson, *Battle Cry of Freedom* (1988); the same author pieces together primary sources to focus on how African Americans felt and acted in *The Negro's Civil War* (1965). Other studies of blacks in the military during this period include Dudley T. Cornish, *The Sable Arm: Negro Troops in the Union Army* (1966); and Joseph T. Glatthaar, *Forged in Battle: The Civil War Alliance of Black Soldiers and White Officers* (1990), which includes excellent appendices listing African-American officers and Congressional Medal of Honor winners. James Hollandsworth, Jr. examines one of the Union's first African American regiments in *The Louisiana Native Guards: The Black Military Experience During the Civil War* (1995); and Noah Andre Trudeau provides an updated, narrative synthesis with useful maps in *Like Men of War: Black Troops in the Civil War, 1862–1865* (1998). Mary Frances Berry's *Military Necessity and Civil Rights Policy: Black Citizenship and the Constitution, 1861–1868* (1977) examines postwar civil rights legislation in the light of black military service.

For primary sources, see Ira Berlin, editor, *The Black Military Experience,* Series II, Volume I of *Freedom: A Documentary History of Emancipation* (1982); and Edwin Redkey, editor, *A Grand Army of Black Men, 1861–1865* (1992), a collection of letters to the editor from black and abolitionist newspapers. C. P. Weaver's *Thank God My Regiment An African One: The Civil War Diary of Colonel Nathan W. Daniels* (1998) is the edited record of the senior commanding officer of the African American 2nd Louisiana Native Guard. More primary sources bearing on the South's quandary may be found in Robert F. Durden, *The Gray and Black: The Confederate Debate on Emancipation* (1972). Jack Fincher, "The Hard Fight Was Getting into the Fight At All," *Smithsonian* 21 (1990): 46–

61 examines both northern prejudices and the concerns of the border states about admitting blacks into the Union army.

Two articles that describe black soldiers' experiences in important battles are Martha M. Bigelow, "The Significance of Milliken's Bend in the Civil War," *Journal of Negro History* 45 (1960): 156–163, and Leonne Hudson, "Valor at Wilson's Wharf," *Civil War Times Illustrated* 37 (1998): 46–52. The issues surrounding the question of the Confederates' treatment of captured black soldiers are explored in several articles. Anne J. Bailey, "A Texas Cavalry Raid: Reaction to Black Soldiers and Contrabands," *Civil War History* 35 (1989): 138–152, finds considerable mistreatment of black Union soldiers in Louisiana and Mississippi. Howard C. Weston, "Captive Black Union Soldiers in Charleston: What To Do?" *Civil War History* 28 (1982): 28–44, focuses on the often conflicting rules and regulations of various offices of the Confederate government and the resulting confusion. "Again in Chains: Black Soldiers Suffering in Captivity," *Civil War Times Illustrated* 20 (1981): 36–43, by Walter L. Williams, examines the treatment of black prisoners of war, free blacks, and slaves during wartime.

Film

The film *Glory* (1990) is available on videocassette and is an excellent look at one African American unit in the Civil War.

CHAPTER 11 (also Volume II, Chapter 1)

Grant, Greeley, and the Popular Press:
The Presidential Election of 1872

The United States is no stranger to vicious presidential elections characterized by bitter personal attacks, grotesque rumormongering, and an incredible level of general nastiness. In 1800 some Federalists charged that, if Thomas Jefferson was elected president, he would confiscate and destroy all Christian bibles. In 1820 a few supporters of Andrew Jackson circulated the rumor that when his opponent John Quincy Adams had been minister to Russia, he had procured pliant women for Tsar Alexander I. In 1884 voters were treated to the embarrassing—and true—accusation that Democratic presidential candidate Grover Cleveland had fathered an illegitimate child ("Ma, Ma, Where's My Pa?" "Gone to the White House, Ha Ha Ha."). And some people claim that the presidential election of 2000 rivaled those earlier contests in viciousness.

There are many theories as to why some presidential elections are replete with personal attacks while others are not (in 1976 candidates Gerald Ford and Jimmy Carter referred to each other as "my distinguished opponent"). Some maintain that the lack of fundamental issues that separate political parties cause those political coalitions to employ personal attacks. Others assert that the divisive issues may be there, but they are potentially so confusing to the electorate that the parties, rather than trust the electorate, attempt to move the voters by using vicious personal charges. And still others claim that an election may be so close (as was 1800, 1884, and 2000) that the respective candidates and parties are afraid to take a stand on any issue that might offend any bloc of voters and instead resort to the lowest common denominator of campaigning. Whatever the answer (and your students may have some idea of their own), there is no question that the presidential election of 1872 between incumbent President Ulysses Grant and Democratic/Liberal Republican challenger Horace Greeley was one of the more vicious and personal in American political history.

The Problem

Content Objectives

1. To learn about the Reconstruction period, and how Reconstruction changed and evolved from 1865 through 1877

2. To understand why Reconstruction failed

3. To use the presidential election of 1872 as a window to understand the Reconstruction period and its political divisions

4. To understand the various options to "solving" the Reconstruction problems offered by the different presidential candidates

Skills Objectives

1. To be able to analyze political cartoons to elicit major issues and controversies as well as the cartoonists' biases

On a larger scale, you might use this chapter to have students think about and discuss one or more of the following questions:

1. Why was the presidential election of 1872 so vicious and filled with personal attacks? Why are *any* elections so vicious?

2. Was Reconstruction a problem with *no* solution? (This discussion inevitably will lead to a question of *choices*, something many historians purposely avoid.)

3. We know that racial issues and racial prejudice in the South *and North* played important roles in the evolution and (perhaps) the ultimate failure of Reconstruction. Did these manifest themselves in 1872? See Volume II, Chapter 2 for African Americans *after* Reconstruction.

Background

We refer students to their text for information on Reconstruction. This section supplements that coverage by examining the political fall of President Andrew Johnson, the rise of General Ulysses Grant and his 1868 election (as shown, Grant was not the naive political neophyte he often has been made out to be), Grant's subsequent difficulties, and the political background to the presidential election of 1872. This section also provides a brief history of illustrated weekly newspapers in the United States and the backgrounds of political cartoonists Matt Morgan and Thomas Nast.

You may wish to provide more background on Horace Greeley, in part because students might get the impression that he was little more than an impractical and fuzzy-minded reformer, and in part because Thomas Nast was so effective in lampooning Greeley. You also might wish to provide more information on Grant, especially to deal with rumors that were played on by Matt Morgan in his cartoons.

The Method

If your students are like ours, they look at political cartoons nearly every day without much knowledge of the issues or events being dealt with or portrayed (most of our students do not read a newspaper with much regularity). Therefore, while we believed that our students were relatively adept at analyzing contemporary cartoons, to our great dismay we discovered that they were not. As a result, we usually choose a contemporary cartoon, transfer it onto a slide or overhead or PowerPoint, and then spend approximately ten minutes or so analyzing that contemporary cartoon when we introduce this problem.

The Method section also offers a brief introduction to students on how to analyze a political cartoon from the past, in this case 1872. We ask our students to read carefully their text's treatment of Reconstruction. While doing so, they are required to make a list of the key issues having to do with Reconstruction in general as well as with the Grant administration, the rebellion of Liberal Republicans, Horace Greeley, and the presidential election of 1872. You might want to check the students' respective lists *before* turning them loose in the evidence.

As students examine the fourteen cartoons in the Evidence section of the chapter, they will see fairly quickly how many of the important issues on their respective lists were *not* dealt with or even addressed in the cartoons. Several issues, however, are addressed. But students may need to make a second list of the issues (or pseudo-issues) addressed in Morgan's and Nast's cartoons. You might want them to see the difference between the *real* issues and events and the *pseudo-issues* and events.

The Evidence

Matt Morgan's cartoons in *Frank Leslie's Illustrated Newspaper* (Sources 1 through 7) can be divided into two clusters: (1) anti-Grant cartoons (Sources 1, 2, 4, 5, 6, and 7) and (2) pro-Greeley cartoons (Sources 2, 3, 5, and 6)—note the overlap of Sources 2 and 5. In Source 1, Grant is depicted as a drunken tool of special interests who are pleading for his favors. Morgan titled the cartoon "Our Modern Belshazzar," an obvious reference to the King of Babylon depicted in the Old Testament Book of Daniel, who while intoxicated saw the "writing on the wall" (Daniel 5: 4–5). In Source 1, the writing on the wall is by B. Gratz Brown: "The times demand an uprising of honest citizens to sweep from power the men who prostitute the name of an honored party to selfish interests." The vast majority of

Americans in 1872 would have been familiar with the story of Belshazzar and the "writing on the wall."

Source 2 shows Greeley (armed with the club "Cincinnati," referring to the site of the Liberal Republican convention) and Carl Schurz rushing to the rescue of Uncle Sam, who is being stripped by Grant of states' rights and by Conkling of congressional independence. The cartoon clearly refers to Liberal Republicans' charges that Grant and the Republicans are turning the federal government into a presidential despotism. And once again there is the "handwriting on the wall," this time by Liberal Republican Senator Lyman Trumball (1813–1896):

> The safety of the citizen, and his protection in his person and property, are to be found in local laws, which the People themselves administer, and not in a central government, where all the powers of the government are combined; and if this system of encroachment is permitted to go on, the day is not distant when our Republican system, based on the idea of a division of powers between the Federal Government and the States, will be transformed into one Imperial despotism, with all power at the City of Washington.

The title of the cartoon in Source 2 is "Uncle Sam in Danger; Or, National Garroters at Work."

Source 3 perhaps is the easiest for your students to analyze. But they will have to know about Greeley's efforts to accommodate the states of the former Confederacy. Again Schurz is assisting.

We have to tell our students the tale of King Canute (c. 994–1035), king of England, Denmark, and Norway. After the students learn the story of the man who came to believe he could order the tides to cease, they have no difficulty with the cartoon in Source 3. As the crown falls from Grant's head, his advisors and hangers-on desert him. In that same vein, Source 5 depicts Grant as an observer of one of his supporters offering an African American man money for his vote (whereas Greeley, in the background, is openly accepting a black man's vote), and in Source 7, Grant, again as the intoxicated despot, turns down the pleas of men he had once commanded and who had raised him to prominence.

In Source 6, Charles Sumner is depicted as the modern-day Moses, with Schurz and Greeley looking on. Sumner (1811–1874) was, by 1872, perhaps second only to Abraham Lincoln as the person most associated with antislavery, emancipation, and African American rights. Students should be reminded that on May 22, 1856, Sumner was assaulted on the Senate floor by South Carolina Congressman Preston Brooks. Prominent in efforts to impeach and remove President Andrew Johnson, Sumner also opposed Grant and was briefly considered as a Liberal Republican presidential nominee. Linking Greeley to Sumner might have been intended to counter Republican attacks on Greeley as too pro-southern ("Let us clasp hands . . .").

Although more detailed than Morgan's efforts, Thomas Nast's cartoons should be easier for your students to analyze. For example, in the cartoon titled "The Republic Is Not Ungrateful" (Source 8), Columbia uses the United States shield to protect Grant from the arrows of "slander," "malice," "misrepresenta-tions," "insinuations," and "lies" loosed by Liberal Republicans and Democrats. Lincoln's bust in the background clearly is meant to depict Grant as the successor to the fallen president.

The remainder of Nast's cartoons selected for this chapter are attacks, many of them vicious, on Greeley and his supporters. In Source 9, Greeley leads a party of men seeking to lure Charles Sumner away from his championing of the rights of African Americans. Note the stark contrast to Morgan's depiction of Sumner as Moses in Source 6. The original size of Source 9 and most of the other cartoons was approximately eleven by fourteen inches. Therefore, reduction of the cartoons to fit on the pages of the students' books may make some things impossible to read. For example, the papers in the black man's hat say "Emancipated by A. Lincoln" and "Protected by U. S. Grant." The schoolhouse in the background is named "Lincoln School." And the ship to which Greeley hopes to take Sumner is called "Democrat" (with "Slavery" marked out and the flags that the ship is flying say "KKK," "Tammany Hall," and "Truce"). You may have to fill in this information so your students can appreciate all of the cartoon in Source 9.

In their books, students will be introduced to the term *allegory* (p. 285). Morgan's cartoons in Sources 1, 4, and 6 are all allegories, as are Nast's cartoons in Sources 9 and 10. It is possible that you may have to familiarize your students with the story of Robinson Crusoe (Source 9) and the Trojan horse (Source 10). Note in Source 10 the image of Greeley's head on the horse and that Schurz has the reins. Note also the figure with KKK on his hat (Nast never missed an opportu-nity to link Greeley to the Klan, as in Source 9).

As noted in the students' books, Nast and others severely misrepresented Greeley's intent when they warped his call to "clasp hands over the bloody chasm." Sources 11 and 13 are only two of Nast's more well-known—and unfair—misrepresentations. The linking of Greeley to John Wilkes Booth and to the Confederates who ran Andersonville prison are perhaps the best examples of how terribly vicious the 1872 presidential campaign was. You may have to help your students with Nast's disgraceful depiction of Abraham Lincoln's tombstone in Source 11 ("The manner of his death is known to all"), a clear insinuation that some supporters of Horace Greeley were responsible for Lincoln's assassination.

In Source 12, Greeley and his allies plot to replace the flag guarded by Uncle Sam with one of their own. Note that the white stripes on the American flag contain the following: "No Secession of States," "Emancipation by Lincoln," "Victory Over the Rebellion," "Honor To Our Union Dead, Honor the Brave," "Rights to All Men, Black and White," and "Freedom of the Press, Speech, and Caricaturing." The flag Greeley is holding, however, has, in part, "Repudiation," "White Supremacy," "This Is a White Man's Government," and "Tammany Democrats Corruption."

As opposed to Nast's cartoon in Source 8 in which Columbia is defending Grant, in Source 14 she is upbraiding Greeley for initially not opposing secession, implying that as commander in chief of the United States Army and Navy, he would not oppose it as president in 1873. "Do you want another Uprising of the North," say the Voice of the People, "a still Bloodier Chasm—more Widows,

Orphans, and Cripples, and another National Debt, you Whited Sepulchre?" The juxtaposition with the monument to those who fought and died to preserve the Union and free the slaves must have been obvious to even the dullest reader, as was the fictional monument's linking of "Lincoln's pen and Grant's sword." As in Source 8, Grant is cast more as a war hero than he is as a president, perhaps for obvious reasons.

Questions to Consider

This section poses questions that will help students to get as much as possible out of each cartoon in Sources 1 through 14. To repeat, students will need your help initially to show them *how* to analyze political cartoons and later to fill in the information that photographic reduction of the cartoons may have made too small or indistinct for students to read (see especially Sources 2, 9, 12, and 14). Usually we pass out photocopies of that material, although lately we have done it on the course's web site.

In this section we pose six questions to help students focus on the sources (you may wish to highlight these questions when you originally introduce the problem):

1. What issue or event is represented in the cartoon?

2. Who are the principal figures and how are they portrayed?

3. What *imagery* is used?

4. Is the cartoon *allegorical* and, if so, what is the basis of that allegory?

5. What *symbols* (flag, Columbia, Uncle Sam, and so forth) are used, and *how* are they used?

6. How were Morgan and Nast trying to influence public opinion?

Questions Students Often Ask

Would Reconstruction have been more successful had Lincoln lived to serve out his second term?

We almost always try to discourage students from asking "what-if" questions. This question, however, has been asked so many times that a number of historians of Reconstruction have dealt with it. In our opinion, the white South and the Radical Republicans were so diametrically opposed to one another's plans for the postwar South that it is difficult to believe that anyone, including Lincoln, would have been able to oversee a Reconstruction that would have satisfied all sides.

Wasn't the real problem the fact that, far from being too harsh, Reconstruction, even congressional reconstruction, was too lenient?

This is a more clearly stated "what-if" question. Many historians of Reconstruction, however, do say that the period was one of lost opportunities, especially with regard to freed African Americans.

Wasn't it more than a bit hypocritical for white northerners to insist that African Americans be allowed to vote in the South when they were still disfranchised in many northern states?

In their behalf, most Radical Republicans favored universal male suffrage everywhere. Other Republicans, however, saw the possibility of building their party in the southern states with black votes. Interestingly, the Republican party in the South today is built on conservative white voters, with most African Americans voting Democratic. In the era under consideration, however, it is true that African Americans cast ballots in South Carolina before they were permitted to do so in New York.

What other foes did Thomas Nast take on in his cartoons?

Although Nast's Reconstruction cartoons probably are his best-known works, he aimed his cartoonists' pen at several other targets. Also well-known are his cartoons against William Marcy "Boss" Tweed and Tammany Hall (whose downfall may be attributed in part to Nast's withering attacks) and the Roman Catholic Church (some of his most vicious work).

Didn't anyone try to get Nast to moderate some of his more vicious cartoons?

Yes. As noted in the students' book (p. 283), *Harper's Weekly* editor George William Curtis "begged the artist to hold his fire." But Nast's cartoons were so popular and probably contributed to the weekly's excellent circulation that owner-publisher Fletcher Harper gave him free rein. When a new publisher took over *Harper's Weekly* and sought to make the magazine less political, however, Nast resigned in a huff in 1886. An attempt to start his own periodical, *Nast's Weekly*, failed.

Epilogue and Evaluation

The Epilogue briefly tells of the hardly surprising outcome of the presidential election of 1872, Greeley's death on November 29, 1872, the waning of Reconstruction fervor, the death of Grant in 1885, and a bit of post-1872 information on Frank Leslie, his widow Miriam Leslie ("Frank Leslie"), and Thomas Nast (students almost always ask what happened to the principal characters in each of our chapters). There is a good deal of information on Miriam Leslie ("Frank Leslie") and you would delight students if you related more of it than is in the students' chapter. She is a fascinating person.

As for evaluation, this chapter virtually begs for giving students another Nast cartoon on 1872 they have not previously seen to analyze, either as an in-class or out-of-class essay or in a group discussion. Some excellent examples may be found in Morton Keller, *The Art and Politics of Thomas Nast* (1968) and J. Chal Vinson, *Thomas Nast, Political Cartoonist* (1967).

For Further Reading

There are a number of superior works on Reconstruction and on Johnson's presidency, too many for all to be listed here. We have found the following the most helpful:

On Reconstruction, especially useful are William R. Brock, *An American Crisis: Congress and Reconstruction* (1963); Dan T. Carter, *When the War Was Over: The Failure of Self-Reconstruction in the South, 1865–1867* (1985); Eric Foner, *Reconstruction: America's Unfinished Revolution, 1863–1877* (1988); John Hope Franklin, *Reconstruction, After the Civil War* (2d ed. 1994); and Patrick W. Riddleberger, *1866, The Critical Year Revisited* (1979).

The best treatment of the election of 1872 is William Gillette's "Election of 1872," in Arthur M. Schlesinger, Jr., ed., *History of American Presidential Elections*, vol. 2 (1971), which also includes some excellent documents to supplement your lecture. Biographical material on the principal candidates may be found in Glyndon G. Van Deusen, *Horace Greeley, Nineteenth-Century Reformer* (1953); William S. McFeely, *Grant, a Biography* (1981); and Jean Edward Smith, *Grant* (2001).

For interesting background on journalism of the period, see Hiley H. Ward, *Mainstreams of American Media History* (1997). On Nast see J. Chal Vinson, *Thomas Nast, Political Cartoonist* (1967) and Morton Keller, *The Art and Politics of Thomas Nast* (1968).

For a new and controversial analysis of the press and presidential elections (unfortunately, only since 1968), see Robert Shogan, *Bad News: Where the Press Goes Wrong in the Making of the President* (2001).

VOLUME II

(For Chapter 1, see page 71.)

CHAPTER 2

The Road to True Freedom:
African American Alternatives in the New South

Some years ago, spurred by an article in the *History Teacher*,[1] we and a number of our colleagues engaged in a long and rather heated discussion about teaching values in our history courses. Although we were aware of increased national interest in this issue, we were surprised by the deep feelings its discussion triggered. References to the Holocaust and to slavery were numerous. Accustomed to treating each other with professional deference, many of us were stunned and confused by the passions our discussion unleashed.

At the risk of oversimplification, the discussion divided us into two nearly equal camps. One group maintained that it was both unfair and unhistorical to judge people of the past using twentieth-century values (such as egalitarianism; respect for the rights of all people; racial, religious, and ethnic equality; and toleration). They argued that historians should neither condemn nor condone, only explain what happened and why. The other group spoke of the purpose of a college or university to reinforce these values, to praise or condemn when appropriate, and to show students that there are higher standards than situational ethics, bare pragmatism, or "if it feels good, do it." Otherwise, this group asserted, we will be turning out of our schools only amoral technocrats, men and women who possess no social sense of right or wrong.

These descriptions, although unfair in their brevity, adequately delineate the two positions. Yet at one point, one of our more reserved colleagues made the following observation (we quote from memory):

> But isn't it true that our courses are *laden* with value judgments, whether we choose to recognize them or not? In fact, how can an examination of history be value free? Just by selecting the people, events, and

---

[1]Margaret Woodhouse and Dan B. Fleming, "Moral Education and the Teaching of History," *History Teacher*, vol. 9, February 1976, pp. 202–209.

trends to talk about, don't we implicitly make value judgments? Maybe what we ought to be doing is *recognizing* what values our courses are communicating (explicitly or implicitly) while at the same time helping our students at least to *recognize* their own values and prejudices.

Of course, he was correct. Whether we choose to admit it or not, we *do* deal with values and, moreover, require that our students do the same. This chapter brings that issue out into the open, where it can be examined and discussed. Students are required to assess the alternatives Ida B. Wells, Booker T. Washington, Henry McNeal Turner, W. E. B. Du Bois, and Francis E. Watkins Harper offered southern African Americans within the context (realities) of the times.

But just as Wells, Washington, Turner, Du Bois, and Harper were products of *their* times, so also are we and our students products of *our* times. Because we did not live in the same period in which these four spokespersons were offering blacks and whites their alternatives, how can we assess which was the best option? And, in this context, what does "best" mean? Most realistic? Most morally defensible? Superior in the long or short range? These questions bring to the surface an issue we purposely excluded from the exercise for the students: historians' subjectivity and how historians' own perceptions of the past are influenced by their own times. You may wish to use this chapter to explore this issue with your students ("Why did you choose the option you did? What does that say about you and your times?").

The Problem

Content Objectives

1. To learn about the efforts of white southerners after Reconstruction to create a "New South" that was imitative of northern industrialization and urbanization

2. To understand why the New South movement was not completely successful

3. To learn what the New South advocates had in mind for African Americans

4. To understand how African Americans were divided on the issue of the best means for achieving racial equality

Skills Objectives

1. To learn how to define terms contained in the central questions historians ask (in this case, to define "best")

2. To be able to identify and understand the differences among the options offered by Wells, Washington, Turner, Du Bois, and Harper

3. To be able to identify a sixth option by analyzing the statistics in Source 7

4. To be able to reach a conclusion about which option was best for African Americans

5. To be able to understand why one has chosen that alternative (optional)

You may also use the chapter to stimulate thought and discussion on a number of broader issues, including the following:

1. Can minorities (whether racial, religious, or ethnic) ever achieve real economic and political gains without the consent (grudging or not) of the majority? If not, how might this be done? If so, how might the majority be influenced to give its consent?

2. Is it necessary for a dispossessed minority to present a united front so as to achieve economic and political gains? Why or why not?

3. How can a person learn more about himself or herself by studying history more introspectively? (Can history teach us about ourselves?)

These questions are both sensitive and difficult. The issue of how reforms are to be effected is a perpetually warm topic among students. Strong feelings may prevent students from giving a fair hearing to the alternatives Wells, Washington, Turner, Du Bois, and Harper offered in light of the realities of the times. For example, students may see Wells's advocacy of economic boycott (by withholding labor and purchasing power) and the arming of African Americans as too confrontational, whereas those same students may discard Washington's position as too timid. Turner's call for a return to Africa and Du Bois's for a "talented tenth" to lead African Americans against injustice may be seen as too impractical, though for quite different reasons. Finally, by emphasizing the crucial role of black women, Harper's "solution" may seem insulting to African American men. Students will be unable to avoid bringing their own feelings about their own times into play. We prefer to confront that problem directly ("What does your statement say about you or the times in which you are living?"), although we make such a confrontation optional in this exercise. You can use this opportunity to help students understand the subjectivity of historians, or you can omit this topic altogether.

Background

The Background section deals with the rise of the New South movement after Reconstruction, a subject not always covered adequately in standard textbooks. Especially stressed here are the goals and thinking of the New South advocates, the less beneficial aspects of the New South movement, and the effects on southern African Americans.

The section concludes with an introduction of several options for African Americans in the South in the late nineteenth century. By touching on the farmers' revolt, we show that African Americans were not merely passive people who were acted on by other people and by historical forces, but were willing to take their destinies into their own hands, as indeed many did. (See Source 7.)

The Method

We discuss this chapter immediately after the one on Reconstruction so that students' focus will remain on the South, but you may want to maintain the chronological flow. If you intend to introduce the optional issue of subjectivity among historians, thereby confronting the question of presentism, it is better to place this chapter in its correct chronological slot.

We find it best for students to begin by defining the terms in the questions they are to answer (see above). Clearly the problem word is "best." In what sense is this word to be used? Does it mean more realistic or achievable? Morally superior? Best in the long or short range? Knowing in advance that this exercise can elicit some very emotional responses from students, we define the task as clearly as we can, warning students of the potential volatility of the issue and explaining that we will discuss the alternatives in an atmosphere of mutual respect.

We then direct the students to the speeches of Wells, Washington, Turner, Du Bois, and Harper and ask them to establish clearly in their minds the alternatives offered by the five speakers. We also ask them to be able to summarize the points that each speaker offers in support of her or his position. You should make clear at the outset that all four spokespersons had the same ultimate goal but differed radically over the means to that end. After the four speakers' alternatives are clear, students should be pointed to Source 7, which shows the beginnings of the massive out-migration of African Americans from the South, a phenomenon that later was called the Great Migration. This will give students a fifth alternative.

Once students have defined the question, analyzed the speeches, and examined the statistics in Source 7, they are ready to choose and defend one of the alternatives as "best." The discussion will be lively, to say the least.

If you decide to use this chapter to explore with students the issue of historians' subjectivity, you will have to introduce the issue in your introductory lecture. We start by explaining very carefully the two principal influences on historians (indeed, on all humans):

1. *Climate of opinion* ("historical time")—a set of values, assumptions, ideas, and emotions shared by people of roughly the same age living at the same time. For example, young people of the 1950s can be characterized as generally cautious, conservative, non-risk takers, and conformists. If we wanted to, we could use the history of the 1950s to explain why most young people shared that climate of opinion. Moreover, we could explain how the climate

of opinion influences the people who share it to react to evidence presented in roughly similar ways.

2. *Frame of reference* ("individual time")—a set of values, assumptions, ideas, and emotions possessed by *one individual*, largely the product of individual experiences (parents, race, gender, growing up, economic situation, formative events). Beatnik poet Allen Ginsberg's stingingly critical reaction to the American materialism and politics of the 1950s was quite different from the reactions of many of his contemporaries, a fact possibly explained by his individual frame of reference.

Every person has both a climate of opinion and a frame of reference, the former shared with others in the society and the latter distinctly his or her own. Every time we listen to music, watch a movie or television, read a book, or examine a painting or piece of sculpture, our climate of opinion and frame of reference together influence our reactions to that experience. The same is true when dealing with historical evidence: our climate of opinion and frame of reference influence how we react to that evidence, what we see in it, and how we interpret it.

To make sure that students understand those concepts, we ask them the following questions:

1. Why does one generation see things differently than another?

2. How can people be influenced by the times in which they live?

3. How does that influence extend to the way they approach the study of the past?

These questions are difficult for those students who are used to getting the "right answers" in other classes. But now it is time they recognize that the right answers for one generation or area may not be the right answers for another time or place. Students also should realize that the person doing the investigating brings to that investigation certain assumptions (formulated by personal climate of opinion and frame of reference). As noted, however, this is an optional part of the exercise and may be omitted; there is no reference to it in the students' text.

The Evidence

The speeches (Sources 1 through 6) are almost self-explanatory. Wells's speech (Source 1) begins with an attack on Henry Grady (see the Background section of this chapter) for his efforts to convince northerners to trust the collective fate of African Americans in the South to southern whites. The result, Wells claims, was lawlessness and lynchings. Wells urged southern blacks, unable to turn to whites (in the North or South) for assistance, to withhold their labor and purchasing power to pressure whites to put an end to the violence. She also advocated that African Americans arm themselves in self-defense.

For his part, Washington was an accommodationist, a gradualist. His belief that African Americans should work for economic progress and defer their demands for political and social rights is clearly enunciated in his Atlanta Exposition Address (Source 2).

At first glance, students will reject Bishop Turner's argument (Source 3) with derision and disgust. Turner's claim that God willed that Africans be brought to America so they could learn about Christianity and a civilization that would elevate them seems strange to students today. However, Turner goes on to say that blacks should embrace that knowledge and return to their African homeland and that the United States government should finance this migration as a repayment for the many decades that slaves labored for nothing. Perhaps the crux of Turner's argument is his opinion that African Americans could never achieve true freedom or equality in a society dominated by whites. Student discussions of Turner's speech often take some rather unusual (and volatile) turns.

Du Bois's "The Talented Tenth" (Source 4) can be seen as a direct attack on Washington's philosophy, as indeed it was. Not only did Du Bois urge that the "best" African Americans earn "traditional" college educations to provide leadership for blacks, but he also believed that such a "talented tenth" could and would be role models for others in the gradual elevation of the race. Furthermore, in his Niagara Address (Source 5), he offers the agenda that the talented tenth should pursue—an immediate end to inequality and discrimination.

For Frances Harper (Source 6), however, the key to improving the African American man is the African American *woman*, a woman who selects a sober and industrious husband, a woman who raises pure, industrious sober *sons*. In the decades following the American Revolution, people spoke and wrote about the crucial role of the "republican mother," who would train her sons for citizenship and leadership in the new nation. Harper's "solution" is not unlike that. If the newly-freed race is to improve itself, Harper asserts, it must do so through its women.

The statistics (Source 7) are almost self-explanatory. Beginning in the 1870s, African Americans increasingly abandoned the states of the former Confederacy for opportunities in the Middle Atlantic, East North Central, and West North Central regions. Although they may have been listening to Wells, Washington, Turner, and Du Bois, at the same time they were "voting with their feet."

Questions to Consider

In the first and second editions of this volume, we included only the speeches of Washington and Du Bois, plus the out-migration statistics. Instructors and students have criticized us for that, explaining that the range of choices was too narrow and that students jumped too quickly to the conclusion that Du Bois was right and that economic progress had been so pitifully slow that Washington's alternative would never have won African Americans their political and social rights. Moreover, armed with hindsight, instructors and students have pointed out that black migration to the North offered African Americans no utopia of freedom and equality of opportunity.

The instructors and students were right. By adding the speeches of Wells, Turner, and Harper, the alternatives students may consider have been enlarged significantly. The addition of Wells also makes Du Bois appear considerably less "radical," and Turner's and Harper's speeches throws Washington into a whole new light—less conservative and more of a "centrist." These changes, however, have made the problem considerably more difficult. In reality, African Americans probably did not choose one alternative over another, but tried a number of options in combinations. The question of the extent to which each alternative would have needed white assistance will prove troublesome.

After examining the evidence, some students will want to discard Wells's alternative as too radical and Turner's and Harper's as too conservative, and then attempt to reach what they feel is a safer middle ground between Washington and Du Bois. Some might select Washington's alternative and then propose that the federal government should have undertaken massive economic assistance programs to speed up the economic uplift process. But was that a realistic alternative, given what most Americans at the turn of the century saw as the proper role of the federal government?

Ultimately, the question of how social change takes place will arise. When students ask you that question, you know the exercise has been successful.

Questions Students Often Ask

How did Henry Grady and his counterparts "sell" industrialization to southerners, long used to agriculture?

Sectional pride was a major component of southern thinking, and Grady used it to good effect. He told the story of the typical southern funeral, in which the shovel and tombstone were products of the North and the only thing the South contributed was "the corpse and the hole in the ground."

Educational opportunities for African Americans and their public school enrollments increased enormously between 1871 and 1880. How did these trends affect the status of African Americans?

Although many African Americans took advantage of educational opportunities, the statistics show that the majority of blacks, except in Mississippi, did not. Schools were segregated, overcrowded, and often staffed by poorly prepared teachers. Literacy, basic arithmetic, and vocational skills were emphasized, and many towns and cities provided only a grammar school education for African Americans before 1900. As a result, it was several generations before educational opportunities offered southern African Americans upward mobility.

Which of the four speakers was most popular among African Americans?
> That is an extremely difficult question to answer. Turner probably had the smallest following (his alternative was the least attractive). Whites believed Washington's supporters were the most numerous, but Du Bois was an increasingly popular figure among African Americans, especially among those men and women with some education. Wells's following was principally among African Americans in the North.

Which of the five speakers had the most white allies?
> As a wheelhorse in the Republican party, Washington had the most powerful white allies, although Du Bois's support among northern white liberals was considerable. Harper had many white women who approved of her position. Wells had numerous white allies, including Jane Addams. Turner had few supporters.

Epilogue and Evaluation

The Epilogue briefly charts the struggle of (and between) African Americans from roughly 1900 to the present. The careers of Wells, Washington, Turner, Du Bois, and Harper are touched on, as is the irony that the so-called New South remained just over the horizon. Grady and others made compromises to help the New South to emerge. What compromises (see the dispute over the Confederate battle flag) will white and black southerners have to make in the future?

Students' feelings and emotions surface in this exercise, so it may be especially difficult to evaluate. At the same time, teachers who believe in clarifying and teaching values cannot fail to use this chapter for their own purposes. Possibilities for evaluation include the following:

1. Ask students to write an editorial evaluating one of the speakers. Divide the class into five sections (one section each writing an editorial on Wells, Washington, Turner, Du Bois, Harper, and the statistics).

2. Set up a debate between supporters of Wells, Washington, Turner, Du Bois, and Harper. Encourage student teams to use your library for additional supporting material.

3. Have students poll other students not enrolled in the class as to the five alternatives. Have them report on the poll and on what it says about the students who were interviewed.

There are many other options, especially if you want to confront the issue of the influences of climate of opinion and frame of reference. Exploring those influences requires imagination and some delicacy.

For Further Reading

Any overview of the post-Reconstruction South must begin with C. Vann Woodward, *Origins of the New South, 1877–1913* (1951). Woodward's seminal work should be supplemented with Roger L. Ransom and Richard Sutch, *One Kind of Freedom: The Economic Consequences of Emancipation* (1977); Jack Temple Kirby, *Darkness at the Dawning: Race and Reform in the Progressive South* (1972); Joel Williamson, *Crucible of Race* (1984); Gavin Wright, *Old South, New South: Revolutions in the Southern Economy Since the Civil War* (1986); Edward L. Ayres, *The Promise of the New South* (1992).

An excellent introduction to African American thought during the period is August Meier, *Negro Thought in America, 1880–1915: Racial Ideologies in the Age of Booker T. Washington* (1963). For the best treatment of Washington see Louis Harlan, *Booker T. Washington: The Making of a Black Leader* (1972). But Washington presently is undergoing considerable historical re-evaluation, and those studies should be appearing very soon, to coincide with the centennial of the appearance of his *Up from Slavery.*

On Wells, see Alfred M. Duster, ed., *Crusade for Justice: The Autobiography of Ida B. Wells* (1970). See also Dorothy Starling, *Black Foremothers* (1979).

On Turner, see Edwin S. Redkey, *Black Exodus: Black Nationalist and Back-to-Africa Movements, 1890–1910* (1969), which places Turner in historical context. See also Stephen Ward Angell, *Bishop Henry McNeal Turner and African-American Religion in the South* (1992).

On Du Bois, see Virginia Hamilton, ed., *The Writings of W. E. B. Du Bois* (1975), which contains most of Du Bois's best work. Recently this has been partially supplanted by the excellent Eric J. Sundquist, ed., *The Oxford W. E. B. Du Bois Reader* (1996). Also on Du Bois, see Shamoon Zamir, *Dark Voices: W. E. B. Du Bois and American Thought* (1995); Kevin F. Gaines, *Uplifting the Race: Black Leadership, Politics, and Culture in the Twentieth Century* (1996).

On Harper, see Francis Smith Foster, ed., *A Brighter Day Coming: A Frances Ellen Watkins Harper Reader* (1990) and Maryemma Graham, ed., *The Complete Poems of Frances E. W. Harper* (1988). The best secondary work is Melba Joyce Boyd's *Discarded Legacy: Politics and Poetics in the Life of Frances E. W. Harper, 1825–1911* (1994).

CHAPTER 3

How They Lived: Middle-Class Life, 1870–1917

The era that began in the last quarter of the nineteenth century and ended after World War I marked the emergence of "modern" American lifestyles. The mail-order catalogue, radio, the movies, and the automobile all broke down regional barriers and fostered an increasingly standardized national culture. Immigrants were "Americanized"; Americans were "homogenized." White middle-class women increasingly were expected to be attractive and companionable wives and mothers in charge of making many of the family's important consumer decisions. Less well-to-do women also were affected by the development of electric appliances and other home products, such as linoleum, which were intended to reduce the drudgery of housework. Furthermore, the American dream of owning one's own home was rapidly becoming a reality for middle-class and skilled working-class families, and residential building was burgeoning. It was an exciting, if confusing, time to live, and the pace of change was both exhilarating and frightening.

The Problem

Although advertisements and commercials pervade our lives, students are not accustomed to thinking about them as historical evidence. In fact, most people are aware of advertising only when it exhibits the most blatant manipulation—these are the commercials people hate. Architecture is even a better example of historical evidence. Nearly all Americans live in private dwellings, whether houses, apartments, or condominiums, but almost no one thinks of a dwelling as evidence that tells a good deal about the time in which it was built and the people who lived in it. In this chapter, students study both advertisements and house plans to learn how Americans used to live and about their hopes and fears.

Content Objectives

1. To learn about the industrialization and urbanization of post–Civil War America

2. To understand the rapid changes in American lifestyles during this era

3. To survey the origins, development, and role of advertising in our society

4. To examine the middle-class values and concerns of the late nineteenth and early twentieth centuries

Skills Objectives

1. To introduce the use of advertisements and house plans as forms of historical evidence

2. To identify the emotional appeals in advertisements and analyze what these advertisements reveal about a society's aspirations and fears

3. To understand how architectural works convey values and impressions to other people

4. To be able to link the values and concerns in advertisements and house plans to the historical trends of the era

Students tend to be "present-minded," and several questions relevant to contemporary life may grow out of this exercise:

1. Many people object to the sexist and racist content of advertisements. What are some of the sex-role stereotypes women complain about? African Americans, often "invisible" in advertisements, are frequently portrayed stereotypically when visible. What are some of those racial stereotypes? Has any of this changed in recent years? If so, how? Why?

2. Young people, especially small children, are subjected to a barrage of television advertising aimed specifically at them. What kinds of advertisements are these? What emotional appeals are used? To what degree do these commercials manipulate young people?

3. Are there any significant differences—in intent and/or technique—between commercial advertisements and public-service messages? Should some advertisements (for guns, liquor, or cigarettes, for example) be banned? If not, why not? If so, how would one determine which advertisements to prohibit?

4. What do present-day suburban homes (or apartment complexes or low-income housing projects) reveal about contemporary society?

Your students also may be concerned about several related issues. For example, students may want to discuss government truth-in-advertising regulations, the wastefulness inherent in the planned obsolescence of annual model and style changes, or advertising's role in creating a demand for unnecessary products. Furthermore, many students are conscious of brand names, particularly in clothing, the "status symbol" aspects of these items, and the importance of peer-group pressure. Occasionally, students on residential campuses want to talk (negatively) about the layout of dormitories (or married student or graduate student housing) and what it tells us about college life. Most students, even the quietest ones, will have something to contribute to this exercise. In fact, your role may be limited to directing the discussion back to the central question: what can these advertisements and house plans tell us about late nineteenth and early twentieth-century middle-class society?

The Method

The entire field of public history has been attracting more attention lately, and some of the most exciting scholarly work has been in the area of material culture: the study of the "built" environment. Works as different as John Demos's pioneering *A Little Commonwealth* and Dolores Hayden's *The Grand Domestic Revolution: A History of Feminist Designs for American Homes, Neighborhoods, and Cities* have contributed to a whole new body of knowledge that helps historians re-create the social and cultural history of earlier Americans. We think that it is important to acquaint students with the historical uses of artifacts previous Americans left behind, and we believe that the period of the late nineteenth and early twentieth centuries is especially appropriate for this introduction.

Our students usually find it easy to analyze the approach of an advertisement—positive, negative, or a combination of both. They find it somewhat more difficult to move beyond their first impressions and look carefully at the entire advertisement. Yet it is important that they see not only *what* is portrayed but *how* it is portrayed. For instance, the size, composition, and functions of family have changed, as well as the roles of family members. Because advertisements often use "ideal" families, students who observe carefully may be able to notice in the advertisements changes in the ideal family (or the lack of such changes) over time.

Early advertisements frequently presented detailed technical information to overcome consumer resistance to new products. Testimonials from "ordinary" people who were satisfied customers served the same purpose (although later advertisements tended to appeal to elitism and hero worship by using testimonials from famous people). In appealing to positive emotions, advertisements touched on patriotism, nostalgia, maternal and paternal feelings, romantic love, ambition, and self-improvement themes. Negative appeals included appeals to feelings of envy, vanity, exclusiveness, anxiety, guilt, and fear.

Many students believe that they do not have sufficient technical expertise to analyze architecture, so for this exercise to be successful, you may have to reassure them. When you lecture on the Gilded Age and the Progressive era, you might wish to emphasize the values and ideas of those times: faith in capitalism, competition, order, efficiency, and so forth. You also might note how these ideas seep into different forms of popular culture, such as the Horatio Alger stories and minstrel shows. Students are then able to recognize that clothing, furniture, houses, and other forms of material culture can reveal the concerns and aspirations of a time period.

The Evidence

The evidence consists of advertisements from Sears Roebuck & Co. catalogues and popular magazines. Sources 1 through 25 give students a general sense of how middle-class Americans lived, as well as more specific information about men, women, children, and families. Sources 26 and 27 are advertisements for owning a home. Sources 28 through 32 are actual house plans and descriptions from pattern books, arranged chronologically.

Questions to Consider

You can approach these advertisements and house plans in several ways. Divide your students into groups and assign each group one question—for example, What do the advertisements tell us about children and young people? That group then goes through all the advertisements, reporting back to the class that there was very little differentiation between boys and girls (clothes and toys, Sources 1 and 2), there were new concerns about health and wholesome entertainment (infant health, magazines, bicycles, and gramophones, Sources 7, 18, and 19), and dating patterns appeared to be changing (Ford Runabout, Source 20). If you use this approach, other questions would focus on women, men, and families.

A second approach is to divide the advertisements among several groups, asking each group to explain what their two or three advertisements reveal. For example, the stove, washer, and vacuum cleaner advertisements (Sources 22 and 23) show that women were solely responsible for housework, how difficult that work was, that many middle-class women had a servant at least part of the time, and that there was great concern about health and cleanliness. The three automobile advertisements (Sources 20 and 21) and the great authors, the correspondence school, and the typewriter advertisements (Sources 14 through 16) are other examples of advertisements that could be clustered this way.

Alternatively, you might wish to use a general discussion to elicit two lists that you then write on the blackboard: values and concerns (or hopes and fears). Students could then use the advertisements to fill in the themes—adequate education, female attractiveness, being up-to-date, and so forth.

The themes of comfort, convenience, beauty, and affordability are evident in the advertisements for buying homes. The advice to a young married couple who wanted to own a home was to live frugally and save (nearly half!) of their income (Source 27). These themes are repeated in the descriptions of the mill hand's cottage (Source 28) and the minister's home (Source 30). An examination of the exterior features of all the houses shows that they are asymmetrical, with towers, cupolas, gingerbread, or other "fancy" features. All have front porches, parlors, three or four family bedrooms, dining rooms, big kitchens with pantries, and sizable entry halls (we call them foyers)—even the mill hand's modest cottage.

Some houses also have additional, special-purpose rooms: sitting rooms, dressing rooms, libraries, nurseries, and servants' bedrooms. Only the house built after 1880 (Source 32) has a bathroom. Students will need to be encouraged to imagine the functions of these rooms. Entry halls were important because they gave visitors their first impression of the home. Some special-purpose rooms were actually larger than other rooms in the house. Parlors, libraries, and dining rooms were formal rooms in which visitors were entertained. Families without live-in servants usually ate their private meals in the kitchen and sat in the sitting room. Front porches were both practical (before air conditioning) and public, in contrast to the more private backyard patio of post–World War II suburban homes. (Like the patio, the family room, den, utility room, and television room or entertainment center are of much more recent vintage.)

Finally, once students have thought about the functions of various special-purpose rooms in these houses, they should try to link the functions with the values and concerns of the era. Some leading questions may help. What do the size and number of bedrooms tell us about families? Why did every house, even the smallest, have a formal entrance, parlor, and dining room? Why were the exteriors of these houses so fancy? What impressions were these homeowners trying to convey to passersby and visitors? Why?

Questions Students Often Ask

Wasn't there any government regulation of advertising during this era?
Until the passage of the Pure Food and Drug Act and Meat Inspection Act in 1906, the general rule was *caveat emptor*—let the buyer beware. Because the worst consumer abuses were found in the meat-packing, canning, and patent medicine industries, these were the first to be regulated. Other products were covered by later amendments to the Pure Food and Drug Act and the Meat Inspection Act, and the Federal Trade Commission (1914) provided further regulatory mechanisms.

How could people afford to buy all these new products?
The huge expansion of the gross national product (40 percent increase between 1919 and 1929) brought consumer prices down while real income rose. New

forms of credit, especially installment buying, also encouraged consumer spending. As a result, private debt increased significantly.

Why were parents so worried about their children?
The growth of towns and cities, the increasing percentage of young people attending high school, and the changing dating patterns brought about by the automobile, movies, and new kinds of music and dancing all worried parents. Many of these changes drew young people away from home and family, and, it was feared, away from traditional moral values.

Was any advertising specifically directed toward young people during this period?
Very little advertising was directed toward children, although boys' magazines carried occasional advertisements for stamps, inexpensive knives, books, or science kits for building things such as crystal sets (radios). There were also a few advertisements for books directed toward girls. However, even advertisements for products that would appeal to teenagers (gramophones, musical instruments, bicycles, games) were aimed at parents rather than young people. Advertisers in this period did not consider children and youths independent consumer groups, and indeed they were not.

How was it possible to keep these houses warm and clean?
Numerous fireplaces and coal furnaces kept houses fairly comfortable, although cooler than most Americans keep their homes today. Residents wore more clothing indoors. Also, heavy draperies kept houses warmer in winter and cooler in summer. Often servants were employed to keep these houses clean, but even so, they were quite a bit dustier and dirtier than today's dwellings. Standards of cleanliness changed dramatically in the 1920s through the 1940s.

Who did the skilled work in building these houses?
Most parts of the houses (doors, windows, columns, gingerbread) were built in shops and transported to the site. However, some work was done by on-site workers. For example, plasterers did the walls and ornate ceilings. (The craft of plastering has all but disappeared today, as have woodcarving and stone carving.)

Why were the ceilings so high? Didn't this cause tremendous heat loss?
Standard ceilings today are eight feet from the floor, but in this era there was no standard ceiling height. Although much heat was lost (people were not so energy conscious), the high ceilings helped circulate the air, an important consideration. As one of our colleagues who lives in an older home has pointed out, high windows let in light in an era when artificial lighting was expensive.

Didn't the publication of house plans and pattern books encourage burglars?
Apparently not.

Epilogue and Evaluation

The Epilogue follows the changes in both values and housing styles up to the present time and also points out that advertising has not lacked its critics and that many of the problems the students have just investigated are still with us. Having analyzed artifacts from an earlier period to determine what they say about a society, students are less likely to accept uncritically the commercials, advertisements, and housing styles being promoted today.

There are several ways to evaluate student performance in this chapter, depending on the number of students in the class, the time available, and your goals for your students. Ask students to write one or two paragraphs analyzing the message of a current advertisement, explaining what the advertisement tells us about our own society. Or ask students, working individually or collectively, to do the same thing in an oral report. Alternatively, you might wish to select an advertisement, reproduce it on an overhead projector or copying machine, and quiz the students about its message.

You also might ask students to bring in a house advertisement from the local newspaper (or provide one yourself for an overhead projector or as a slide) for analysis. In writing-emphasis courses, have students write a blurb for a middle-class house advertisement to be published in either 1880 or 1910. Depending on your situation, you and your students might visit a historic home near your campus.

For Further Reading

There has been a real explosion of scholarship recently that focuses on the development and growth of our modern consumer economy. Useful older scholarship includes Edgar R. Jones, *Those Were the Good Old Days* (1950), and Frank Rowsome, Jr., *The Laughed When I Sat Down* (1959), both of which are well-illustrated, narrative histories of advertising. Good overviews of the growth of consumerism include Daniel Horowitz, *The Morality of Spending: Attitudes Toward the Consumer Society in America, 1875–1940* (1985); Susan Strasser, *Satisfaction Guaranteed: The Making of the American Mass Market* (1989); Pamela W. Laird, *Advertising Progress; American Business and the Rise of Consumer Marketing* (1998); Regina L. Blaszcznyk, *The Rise of Consumer Society, 1865–1945* (2000). The work of T. Jackson Lears is particularly valuable, especially the edited collection, *The Culture of Consumption* (1983), and his wide-ranging *Fables of Abundance: A Cultural History of Advertising* (1994).

David Blanke, *Saving the American Dream: How Consumer Culture Took Root in the Rural Midwest* (2000) is a regional study that is especially insightful on the role of the Grange, the rural ethos, and the formation of mail-order houses. William Leach's, *Land of Desire* (1993) is the standard source about the rise of the urban department store, and Lendol Calder's *Financing the American Dream: A*

Cultural History of Consumer Credit (1999) provides a detailed overview of the development of various credit options between 1870 and 1940.

Mass circulation magazines played an important role in the growth and nationalization of consumerism during the late nineteenth and early twentieth centuries. Mark Schneirov, *The Dream of a New Social Order: Popular Magazines in America, 1893–1914* (1994) examines popular middle class magazines such as *Cosmopolitan* and *McClure's*, Jennifer Scanlon, *Inarticulate Longings* (1995) specifically analyzes the influence of the *Ladies' Home Journal*. Ellen G. Garvey, *The Adman in the Parlor: Magazines and the Gendering of Consumer Culture, 1880s–1910s* (1996), includes a discussion of ad writers, contests, and trade cards as well as magazines in general. The influence of the customers' gender upon design, marketing strategies, and production processes during this time period are among the topics in Roger Horowitz and Arwen Mohun, eds., *His and Hers: Gender, Consumption, and Technologies* (1998).

Wayne Andrews, *Architecture, Ambition and Americans* (rev. ed. 1978); David Handlin, *The American Home: Architecture and Society, 1815–1915* (1980); Gwendolyn Wright, *Moralism and the Modern Home* (1980); *Building the American Dream* (1981); and Clifford Clark, *The American Family Home* (1986), all offer useful overviews of the relationships between home styles and American society during this era. Harvey Green, *The Light of the Home: An Intimate View of the Lives of Women in Victorian America* (1983) is a wonderful study of Victorian homes and the values they communicated. For a look at how the "other half" of the people lived, see Jared Day, *Urban Castles: Tenement Housing and Landlord Activism in New York City, 1890–1943* (1999), which is especially good on the evolving designs, cost-cutting, and crowding of the tenements.

New scholarship also tends to focus on the material culture of the era, including the uses of space, choice of furnishings, and other objects in the home such as toys and appliances. Simon Bronner has written several good books on material culture; especially helpful for this chapter is his edited collection, *Consuming Visions: Accumulating and Display of Goods in America, 1880–1920* (1989). Thomas Schlereth, *Victorian America: Transformations in Everyday Life* (1991), and Jessica Foy and Thomas Schlereth, eds., *American Home Life, 1880–1920* (1992) provide excellent examples of the material culture approach to social history.

Video

America 1900, produced by David Grubin, 1998. 175 minutes. This video is part of *The American Experience* series, and establishes the major historical figures and events of the turn of the century. Teachers' aids such as maps and timelines, additional primary sources, and a topically arranged bibliography are available at the Public Broadcasting web site: http://www.pbs.org/wgbh/pages/amex/1900.

CHAPTER 4

Justifying American Imperialism:
The Louisiana Purchase Exposition, 1904

Like other Western nations, the United States somehow has always needed to justify its imperialistic ventures. Whether its ventures were against American Indians, Mexicans, Africans, Asians, or peoples of the Middle East, westerners (including the United States) in the late nineteenth century constructed a complex set of arguments to make it seem, if only to themselves, that these forays were economically and morally correct.

How the American government justified its building of a modest empire is the subject of this chapter. The St. Louis Exposition of 1904 was a matchless opportunity for the United States government to justify its colonial expansion to the world and, more importantly, to its own people. By displaying several peoples (including Native Americans, Eskimos, and Filipinos) in simulations of their native habitats, the United States could demonstrate the extent to which it had "rescued" these peoples from barbarism and heathenism. Alongside exhibits of Western technology, the exhibits of the Anthropology Department revealed the stark differences between the lives of industrial and preindustrial peoples. The assumption was that the United States would bring the "blessings" of civilization to the peoples within its sphere. The more barbarous these peoples could be portrayed, the more obvious (it was assumed) it was that they needed the protective arm and guidance of their new masters.

Thus in some ways, the anthropology exhibits at the 1904 exposition were manipulated or staged events, seeking to elicit a specific reaction from Western visitors. In that sense, they were a marvelous success.

The Problem

Content Objectives

1. To learn about how the United States, along with other Western nations, participated in the imperialist scramble for territories in the late nineteenth century

2. To learn how the United States sought to justify this imperialism to both its own people and the world

Skills Objectives

1. To be able to analyze photographic evidence as to content, intent, message, and bias (in other words, to be able to "read" photographs)

2. To be able to look beyond the surface messages of photographs (or other evidence) to see the *subliminal* messages therein

It would be wrong to suggest that the St. Louis exhibitors were cynical and calculating in what they chose to show, or not show, the fair's visitors. Most of the exhibitors believed that they had arranged an objective portrait of Philippine society, yet, intentionally or unintentionally, this was far from the case. As a larger question, you might ask your students why so few people perceived this failure. Were the cultural or ethnocentric "blinders" too strong?

On a similar note, many people who toured the Philippine Reservation must have felt sorry for most of these peoples (as they must have when viewing Native Americans or Eskimos). Yet what reaction is sympathy likely to produce, whether it be in 1904 or 2004? In that sense, isn't sympathy a powerful weapon for intervention in the political, economic, and cultural lives of the downtrodden? As you raise these questions, students will very quickly scan their own attitudes about other peoples in the 2000s.

Background

The Background section touches briefly on the reasons Western nations, including the United States, embraced imperialism in the late nineteenth century. Especially stressed are competition between Western nations; technological improvements in transportation, communications, medicine, and weaponry; a new climate of opinion in the business community; missionary zeal; and new "scientific" arguments that tended to support social Darwinism and the "white man's burden." You may want to highlight these points yourself, adding your own thoughts on the subject. Indeed, one of our colleagues emphasizes what he calls the psychosexual reasons for imperialism—that is, the failure of Western males to fulfill their economic duties and their transference of this "defect" to "manly" imperialism. Background on the Spanish-American War of 1898 also is provided. The section concludes by returning to the St. Louis Exposition, principally to refocus students on their primary task.

The Method

Students often believe that, unlike paintings, drawings, or sculpture, photographs are objective and completely neutral depictions of reality. Before they begin to examine and analyze the evidence in this chapter, therefore, students must understand that photographic evidence is *not* objective but instead filled with biases. The objects to be photographed are selected with a particular purpose or view in mind. The photographer also can have biases when "recording" the event. The following questions will help students work through the evidence:

1. What is the photographer's "message"?

2. How (if at all) is the photographer biased?

3. How are buildings, people, clothing, and other objects used in the photograph to convey the message?

Students may not be used to viewing photographs with a critical eye, especially regarding photographs' messages. After all, aren't photographs "real" or objective evidence? In fact, few are. Most photographs (including those in family albums) are designed to convey certain messages.

On one occasion, we showed our students photographs by Lewis Hine about the depression of the 1930s. We now know that these photographs were staged. What impression does the photographer want to convey? Any similar photographic collection will do, as long as you can demonstrate that a photograph is a subjective piece of evidence—often arranged and posed, often taken for emotional effect.

The Evidence

Sources 1 through 3 are examples of some of the impressive and ornate buildings on the fair site (notice the enormous Ferris wheel in the background in Source 3). Clearly these buildings were intended to be juxtaposed against the "primitive" buildings and peoples brought to the exposition by the Anthropology Department. These buildings were what "civilized" people could construct. As visitors toured the Anthropology Department, they must have been impressed by the contrast, which was the intention of the fair's organizers.

Sources 4 through 11 were designed to place most Filipinos in a lower order, indicating that they needed the "civilization" that American imperialism could bring. Source 4 (a painting prominently displayed at the exposition) depicts the inherent racism and ethnocentrism of the Anthropology Department and, indeed, of the vast majority of white Americans. Sources 5 through 11 show photographs of selected Filipinos in what was assumed were their normal states of "barbarism" (the nickname in Source 5 is particularly offensive). Students will have no difficulty imagining how Western visitors would have responded to scenes of Tagalo women washing, Igorots dancing and preparing a feast of dog, and Bontoc head-hunters.

Sources 12 through 14 are photographs of Westernized Filipinos. Ask students why the Visayans would have been invited to the exposition. Source 14 is especially instructive, since it shows part of the process of Westernization. Ask students about the goals of any educational process.

Source 15 is an excerpt from an article by W. J. McGee, head of the Anthropology Department. Notice how similar McGee's thinking was to that of the artist who created the painting in Source 4. But McGee had to go one step further: as an obvious Darwinian, he had to explain why "barbaric" people continued to exist side by side with "superior" humans. For McGee's own cultural biases, see especially the last two paragraphs of the excerpt.

Questions to Consider

This section asks questions that will help students reflect on the photographs and on McGee's excerpt. We have found it effective to refer back to Sources 1 through 3 (the Western buildings and people) regularly while taking students through Sources 4 through 14.

Students will see very quickly the message of the Anthropology Department specifically and the exposition in general: if people accepted Western ways, they were considered to be on the "road to civilization" and hence were lauded (the Visayans, for instance). If people did not accept Western ways, more effort would have to be made to convince them to do so, to become (as they were called) "objects of civilization." McGee's excerpt, however, expresses some implied doubt that the process of "civilization" would ever be complete.

Questions Students Often Ask

Did the Filipinos ever protest the ways they were portrayed at the exposition?
Evidence is lacking in this area, but apparently there was disgruntlement among some of the Filipinos, principally over required dress codes and when some Filipinos became ill. We do not have much information on this subject.

Did any Americans object to the Philippine Reservation?
Again, evidence is virtually nonexistent. Objections would have been reported. After all, anti-imperialists could have used the exhibitions in their own way, to argue that these peoples would never be able to become part of the United States. Interestingly, some early visitors to St. Louis did object to some Filipinos' lack of clothing. As a result, exposition officials required Filipinos to wear clothing that some of them would not normally have worn.

Because the Anthropology Department at St. Louis was so popular, was it repeated at subsequent expositions?
    Indeed it was, although not on as large a scale as that of the 1904 exposition.

Epilogue and Evaluation

The Epilogue brings the history of the Philippines to the fall of the Marcos regime in 1986 and traces the changing nature of world's fairs in the United States. Students should get the point that, in spite of the United States' genuine efforts to bring the Philippines gradually to self-government, politics in the Philippines after 1946 has been marked by instability. Students might want to ruminate on the causes of political volatility in the nation. Had the United States done all it could to prepare the Philippines for self-government? Was the economic situation in the Philippines working against political democracy and popular participation?
    Methods for evaluating students' work in this chapter are numerous and varied, limited only by your own goals:

1. Based on the photographic evidence, students can write a newspaper account of the 1904 exposition as if they had visited the fair, especially pointing out the Philippine Reservation.

2. Students can "open up" this exercise if they are given photographs of non-Filipinos who were also "on display" at the exposition (Source 16, a photograph of Sioux men, women, and one child). This would make for an extremely interesting discussion.

3. Students can debate whether or not the Anthropology Department should have created such a display.

For Further Reading

The material on American imperialism is varied and excellent. Walter LaFeber's *The New Empire: An Interpretation of American Expansion* (1969) argues that this phenomenon was the "natural culmination" of American entrepreneurial and Turnerian thought. Lloyd C. Gardner's *Imperial America: American Foreign Policy Since 1898* (1976) is a critical view of American involvement, with an excellent section on the paradox of American imperialism. H. Wayne Morgan's *America's Road to Empire* (1965) concentrates on the period prior to 1900. For one view on teaching American imperialism see James A. Field, "American Imperialism: The 'Worst Chapter' in Almost Any Book," *American Historical Review*, vol. 83 (June 1978), pp. 644–683. Additional arguments are made by Michael L. Krenn, *Race and U.S. Foreign Policy in the Ages of Territorial and Market Expansion, 1840–1900* (1998) and Mansour Farhang, *U.S. Imperialism: The Spanish-American War to* the *Iranian Revolution* (1993). For a view of European imperialism see Mark Cocker, *Rivers of Blood, Rivers of Gold: Europe's Conquest of Indigenous Peoples* (2001).

For background on the Philippines, we recommend Leon Wolff, *Little Brown Brother* (1961); Peter Stanley, *A Nation in the Making: The Philippines and the United States, 1899–1921* (1974); Anne C. Kwantes, *Presbyterian Missionaries in the Philippines: Conduits of Social Change, 1899–1910* (1989); and Nick Culla-thar, *Illusions of Influence: The Political Economy of United States–Philippine Relations, 1942–1960* (1994).

As for world's fairs in general and the St. Louis Exposition in particular, see Robert W. Rydell, *All the World's a Fair: Visions of Empire at American Interna-tional Expositions, 1876–1916* (1984). A multivolume primary source on the 1904 exposition is J. W. Buel, ed., *Louisiana and the Fair: An Exposition of the World, Its People, and Their Achievements* (1904). For a superb new survey of the 1904 exposition (with several previously unpublished photographs of Philippine peoples) see Timothy J. Fox and Duane R. Sneddeker, *From the Palaces to the Pike: Visions of the 1904 World's fair* (1997).

On photography see Beaumont Newhall, *The History of Photography from 1839 to the Present* (rev. ed. 1982) and Susan Sontag, *On Photography* (1977 ed.).

On nineteenth-century science and race, see Stephen J. Gould, *The Mismea-sure of Man* (1981).

CHAPTER 5

Homogenizing a Pluralistic Nation: Propaganda During World War I

In his autobiography, former chairman of the Committee on Public Information George Creel recalled,

> What I proposed was the creation of an agency that would make the fight for what Wilson himself had called "the verdict of mankind"; an agency that would not only reach deep into every American community, clearing away confusions, but at the same time seek the friendship of neutral nations and break through the barrage of lies that kept the Germans in darkness and delusion. . . . From the first, nothing stood more clear than the confusion and shapelessness of public opinion. The country as a whole accepted the war, but there was no complete under-standing of it as a war of self-defense that had to be waged if free insti-tutions were not to go down under the rushing tide of militarism.[1]

Creel vehemently denied that the committee manipulated public opinion ("A free people were not children to be humored, cajoled, or lollipopped"), but it is clear from this excerpt that he was a man of strong feelings and prejudices that in-evitably affected the committee's task of uniting public opinion behind the war effort. Indeed, fellow journalist Mark Sullivan once wrote of Creel:

> For such a job Creel is the most unsuitable of men. President Wilson might just as appropriately have appointed Billy Sunday. Indeed, George Creel and Billy Sunday have much in common. What Sunday is to religion Creel is to politics. Creel is a crusader, a bearer of the fiery cross. His ten years as a newspaper man in Kansas City and five in Denver were devoted to the championship of one form after another of idealism.

---

[1]George Creel, *Rebel at Large: Recollections of Fifty Crowded Years* (New York: G. P. Putnam's Sons, 1947), pp. 156–175.

Sullivan may have been unfair. But there is little doubt that Creel's own views about "a unified front" were important in the operation of the Committee on Public Information.

The Problem

Content Objectives

1. To understand why the United States became involved in World War I and the nation's ultimate contributions to an allied victory

2. To learn about life on the home front during the war (government regulations, war production, propaganda and civil liberties, racial issues, and so forth)

3. To understand why the Wilson administration created the Committee on Public Information, what the committee did, and how the committee contributed to the homogenization of and hysteria within American society

Skills Objectives

1. To be able to identify various propaganda techniques and the real feelings or fears on which they are playing

2. To be able to use songs, posters, speeches, and film reviews as pieces of historical evidence

On a larger scale, this chapter may be used to raise a number of questions and issues for thought and discussion, including the following:

1. What is "total war"? Why are civilians so important in modern wars?

2. To what extent should civil rights be restricted or suspended in wartime? Should antiwar protests (which, some people would say, encourage the enemy and demoralize our people) be allowed?

3. To what extent should the government have the power to mold public opinion during wartime? Is there any danger that such activity might carry over into peacetime?

4. How much control should government have over the press during wartime? During peacetime? Is irresponsible journalism (during war or peace) a problem? If so, how can that irresponsibility be dealt with?

Background

Post-Vietnam era students, who have had a lifelong exposure to the influences of mass media advertising, are certain to find the problem of wartime propaganda interesting and challenging. To analyze the propaganda efforts of the Committee on Public Information, students will need to understand clearly the factors that kept the United States out of the war until 1917, as well as the economic, political, and social factors that drew the nation into the conflict. You will probably cover these topics in earlier lectures, but the following points should be re-emphasized to facilitate the discussion:

1. Prior to the United States' entry into the war, the American people strongly supported the policy of neutrality and isolation President Wilson espoused.

2. At the same time, strong economic and commercial ties bound the nation to Europe, particularly to the Allied powers.

3. American policy was never entirely neutral but reflected the nation's ethnic ties to the Allied powers and the pro-British sentiments of Wilson and his advisers.

4. Americans were adversely affected by the naval blockades of both belligerents, but they were particularly critical of the developments in submarine warfare the Germans had made. Although the German policy of unrestricted submarine warfare did not force the Americans into a declaration of war, it pushed the nation toward involvement.

5. The interception and publication of the Zimmermann telegram affected public opinion in America.

6. The United States entered into the conflict despite the lack of clear-cut aggressive action by the Central Powers against the country and government fears about public support for the war effort.

The Method

Depending on how much you do with it, this exercise can be comparatively simple or quite complicated. The evidence can be analyzed to different degrees. For example, several of the posters use sexual innuendoes and the image of American males as masculine figures. How deeply you have your students dig into the evidence is up to you.

　　To help students examine the evidence, we list four general goals of American propaganda during World War I, five features of effective World War I propaganda, and the following five questions that students must ask of each piece of evidence:

1. For whom was this piece of propaganda designed?

2. What was this piece of propaganda trying to get people to think? To do?

3. What logical appeal was being made?

4. What emotional appeal(s) was being made?

5. What might have been the results, positive and negative, of these kinds of appeals?

As students go through the evidence, they should make notes to help them answer each of the five questions. Those notes will be extremely useful when they look for common themes, appeals, and images and attempt to answer the two central questions: (1) How did the United States use propaganda to mobilize public opinion during World War I? (2) What were some of the positive and negative consequences of this type of propaganda? (Students will be able only to guess at an answer at first, but the Epilogue will help fill in much of the information.)

The Evidence

The evidence is grouped by type: lyrics from one popular song, three advertisements, nine posters, two editorial cartoons, three excerpts from speeches delivered by and poems read by Four Minute Men, an advertising aid for the commercial film *Kultur,* a photograph of a scene from the New York premiere of *The Kaiser: The Beast of Berlin,* one promotional "still" from that film, and a movie poster advertising the film *The Prussian Cur.* Each propaganda form offers the propagandist a number of possibilities but places certain restrictions on his or her work. For example, songs had to convey their messages rather quickly, whereas advertisements could be read and studied at a more leisurely pace and hence could be expected to do more things. Posters are the visual counterparts of songs, having to make a rapid impression on viewers. The speeches were created for audiences who would hear them only once. This does not mean that the songs or posters could not contain some rather subtle and even unconscious appeals, only that the connections in the listeners' or viewers' minds had to be made almost instantaneously.

Lyrics from Popular Song

George M. Cohan's "Over There" (Source 1) is probably the most popular song to come from World War I. Complete with rousing tune, "Over There" was intended to excite the listeners (especially males) and make them want to volunteer for service. In addition to the patriotic theme, there is much more in the song: father, sweetheart, mother—all will be proud of the volunteer. In one sense, then, "Over There" also was an appeal to these people: do not discourage or block the volunteers; support their courageous impulses to join the battle.

Committee on Public Information Advertisements

In Sources 2 through 4, three Committee on Public Information (CPI) advertisements ("Spies and Lies," "Bachelor of Atrocities," and "What Can History Teachers Do Now?") have been reproduced. On the surface, "Spies and Lies" was a simple appeal not to pass information unwittingly to the enemy, but it was much more too. For example, what kind of information is mentioned ("malicious, disheartening rumors")? What kind of behavior is suggested (say nothing and report rumormongers)? Ask your students how this kind of appeal might have gotten out of hand. Should Americans not communicate true events (e.g., a military defeat) to one another?

"Bachelor of Atrocities" was a frank request for college graduates to buy liberty bonds. But the appeal is most interesting. How are the Germans portrayed? How have they "ruined" warfare? The Germans destroyed the University of Louvain because it was a military obstacle to their invasion of France. How did the Committee on Public Information use this event? What about the careful choice of words (like the "vicious guttural language of Kultur")?

"What Can History Teachers Do Now?" will elicit a great deal of discussion, in part because many students read history books (including this one) as if they were completely objective. And yet the CPI advertisement "What Can History Teachers Do Now?" actually encourages teachers to tilt American history and present a subjective opinion as if it were fact. This advertisement has caused a near-riot in our classrooms when students come to understand that history can be used as a weapon in the interests of governmental policy. This discussion will be more than stimulating.

Posters

Sources 5 through 13 are representative of the hundreds of posters created to encourage certain behavior. All of these posters either were commissioned or approved by the CPI. In many cases (Sources 6 and 7 are representative) the enemy was depicted as brutes or rapists. Along with Cohan's song "Over There," the posters made specific appeals to American masculinity (see also the cartoon in Source 15, the poem in Source 18, and the still photograph from the film in Source 21).

The Joan of Arc image (Source 8) must have been especially exciting to American women because it contains implied *activity*, not passivity. What were women on the "home front" expected to do? How (if at all) would they be rewarded? The woman Columbia is also the principal figure in the poster depicted in Source 9 ("Be Prepared"). Ask your students how Columbia is depicted.

Given the CPI's concern about whether people of different ethnic backgrounds would support the war effort, Sources 10 through 13 are of particular interest (Sources 11 through 13 are new in this edition). The appeal for homogeneity is clear, and students will have no difficulty with the less-than-subtle message. How did such an appeal resonate in the American community, especially with regard to German-Americans?

Cartoons

Students will easily see the message of the *New York Herald* cartoon (Source 14). We try to get them to imagine whether, seeing this cartoon for the first time in 1918, they would have felt hatred for Dr. Muck alone or for other Germans and German-Americans as well.

Source 15 is a prize-winning cartoon from a U.S. serviceman. One assumes that the German from whom the American soldier has taken the *pickelhaube* has been killed. What does this cartoon tell your students about the American concept of total victory? Look at the adoring eyes of the serviceman's family.

Four Minute Men Speeches and Poem

Most important in the Four Minute Men speeches are the images being conveyed. The shocking beginning of Source 16 ("there is a German spy among us") set up the audience for what the speaker really intended to do: make them feel afraid not to contribute and make them hate the enemy enough to want to contribute. The approach must have been very effective.

Source 17 also plays on fear, but of a different kind. The audience appears to have been white ("they will not oppose" instead of "you will not oppose"). What, then, is the fear that the speaker was trying to elicit? The late nineteenth and early twentieth centuries saw a marked increase in racism in the United States. How did this excerpt play on that feeling? Could such emotions get out of hand?

The poem "It's Duty Boy" (Source 18) pleads for parents to let their sons go to war. Note that the son, even if he were killed, would raise the parents' status. What of those sons who refused to serve?

Commercial Films

Since their inception, motion pictures often have been able to elicit strong emotions from their viewers. This fact was not lost on the CPI, which produced numerous documentary films and short subjects and acted as a censor on commercial films produced during World War I.

The commercial film *Kultur*, according to the advertising aid provided by the studio publicist (Source 19), used sexual innuendoes to portray the kaiser and other Germans as insatiable beasts and men who would stoop to any level to achieve their ends. Notice the phrases "Gave Her All for Democracy" and "Hun Plots to Rape Democracy."

Unfortunately, no prints of *The Kaiser: The Beast of Berlin* exist. Judging by the photograph used in the advertisement (Source 20), the film must have been immensely popular—a literal traffic jam on Broadway. Source 21 provides one clue as to why the film was so popular: the rapacious German lusting after a young woman and her mother (grandmother?), protected only by the masculine hero of the Allies. A similar portrayal of Germans can be seen in Source 22: the kaiser as butcher of women. This time the depiction of the hero is more obvious. *Kultur, The Kaiser: The Beast of Berlin,* and *The Prussian Cur* all were extremely popular films. No prints of any of these "movies" exist.

Questions to Consider

The questions help students delve below the surface messages of the evidence to the deeper— and often more compelling—appeals. Some of our students have been enthusiastic about doing this, but others have remained somewhat reticent. Once the ice has been broken, most of our students are able to see both the surface and hidden appeals. They also are willing to talk about how modern advertising techniques (automobile advertising, for example) are an improvement over the comparatively crude work of the Committee on Public Information.

Questions Students Often Ask

Did other belligerents use posters?
> Yes, although on a less massive scale than the United States. Through the third liberty loan drive, more than 16 million posters were distributed.

Did other nations use posters to elicit hatred of the enemy?
> Interestingly, German and Austrian posters were virtually free of this hatred. British, American, and French posters often used threats of "the Hun." German and Austrian posters emphasized patriotism.

Were American artists paid for creating these posters?
> No. They donated their time and talents, as did actors and other entertainers.

How many Four Minute Men were there?
> By the end of the war, approximately seventy-five thousand speakers were registered as Four Minute Men by the Committee on Public Information.

Did any women serve as Four Minute Men?
> Yes. Women addressed audiences at matinees and women's clubs. There also was a Junior Four Minute Men movement in the schools and a Colored Division that recruited African Americans to speak to black audiences.

How many movie theaters were there in the United States during World War I?
> In 1921, the United States had approximately 16,900 movie theaters. It is not known how many were operating during World War I.

Epilogue and Evaluation

The Epilogue traces how Americans embraced this propaganda, until the anti-German fervor eventually got out of hand and something akin to a national hysteria was created. It is doubtful whether this effect was what Creel had intended. However, as seen from the committee-sponsored evidence in this chapter, those reactions might have been anticipated.

The chapter can be evaluated in a number of ways:

1. Ask students to write a set of guidelines for a World War I poster, indicating what surface and hidden appeals should be used and how.

2. Have students write a letter to the editor either for or against the Committee on Public Information.

3. Have students write an essay on how the Committee on Public Information attempted to "unify" the country during World War I.

4. Conduct a debate about whether the Committee on Public Information was or was not an indispensable part of government during World War I.

5. Bring some additional evidence to class and have students work with it the way they worked with evidence in this exercise. Source 24, a poster from World War II, also may be used for this purpose.

For Further Reading

George Creel, *How We Advertised America* (1920). The story of the Committee on Public Information; informative but self-serving.

James R. Mock and Cedric Larson, *Words That Won the War: The Story of the Committee on Public Information, 1917–1919* (1939), and James R. Mock, *Censorship 1917* (1941). Both are helpful, slightly sympathetic to the committee, and not as analytical as they should be. Harry N. Scheiber's *The Wilson Administration and Civil Liberties, 1917–1921* (1960) is better, and Stephen L. Vaugh's *Holding Fast the Inner Lines: Democracy, Nationalism, and the Committee on Public Information* (1979) is much better.

Arthur S. Link, *Woodrow Wilson: Revolution, War and Peace* (1979). Part of a multivolume biography of Wilson; excellent in providing background and context.

Alfred E. Cornebise, *War as Advertised: The Four Minute Men and America's Crusade, 1917–1918* (1984). Examines the work of the roughly seventy-five thousand speakers the Committee on Public Information enlisted.

Michael T. Isenberg, *War on Film: The American Cinema and World War I, 1914–1941* (1981). Contains interesting information on both documentaries and commercial films.

Creighton Peet, "Hollywood at War," *Esquire,* September 1936, pp. 60, 109. A highly critical look at World War I films. Peet feared a revival of this type of film as a result of the worsening international situation in the 1930s.

David Kennedy, *Over Here: The First World War and American Society* (1980). An excellent analysis of the home front. For some interesting primary material on that topic, see David F. Trask, ed., *World War I at Home: Readings on American Life, 1914–1920* (1970).

Robert C. Hilderbrand, *Power and the People: Executive Management of Public Opinion in Foreign Affairs, 1897–1921* (1982). Especially informative on the role of Wilson in the management of public opinion.

Charles De Benedetti, *The Peace Reform in American History* (1985), and Charles De Benedetti, ed., *Peace Heroes in Twentieth Century America* (1986). The two works outline antiwar efforts and the lives of the participants, including Jane Addams and Eugene Debs.

Craig W. Campbell, *Reel America and World War I: A Comprehensive Filmography and History of Motion Pictures in the United States 1914–1920* (1985). A valuable research book of cultural history outlining the development of filmmaking from entertainment to its use by political forces.

Clayton R. Koppes and Gregory D. Black, *Hollywood Goes to War: How Politics, Profits, and Propaganda Shaped World War II Movies* (1987). A source for comparison between the two wars.

William G. Jordan, *Black Newspapers and America's War for Democracy, 1914–1920* (2001) argues that African American newspapers were less accommodationist than heretofore believed.

Film

To locate World War I era films, we recommend Patricial King Hanson, exec. ed., *The American Film Institute Catalog of Motion Pictures Produced in the United States,* vol. FI, *Feature Films, 1911–1920* (Berkeley, 1988).

The film *Goodbye Billy: An American Goes to War, 1917–1918* was recommended to us as containing additional evidence. The film was produced in 1974 and is twenty-nine minutes long. A study guide accompanies the film.

CHAPTER 6

The "New" Woman: Social Science Experts and the Redefinition of Women's Roles in the 1920s

Americans who came of age after World War II, the so-called "television genera-tion," are apt to base much of their historical awareness on mass media presenta-tions. Our current students, bombarded with images from television, video games, and the Internet, are even more vulnerable to stereotypical or ahistorical visions of the past. Both the 1920s and the 1960s have been treated extensively and super-ficially by the mass media; the women who came of age in those decades are usually presented as Jazz Age flappers or hippie flower children.

Yet historians know that in both the 1920s and the 1960s very complex, although incomplete, redefinitions of women's roles were actually occurring. In this chapter, we want to encourage the students to examine the changing ideas about women's place during the decade of the 1920s. Specifically, we want stu-dents to evaluate the influence of the new social science "experts" on the redefini-tion of women's roles.

The Problem

The conflict between modernism and the values and beliefs of an older, rural America was brought into sharp relief by the growth of the consumer economy, the emergence of a mass culture, and the candidacy of Alfred E. Smith in 1928. Many of these changes had their roots in the pre–World War I era, and the earliest emergence of the "new" woman was welcomed because she seemed to retain the traditional virtues associated with motherhood. Female Progressive reformers emphasized that they simply wanted to apply their maternal virtues to solving problems that were connected with, but outside of, the purely domestic sphere. By the 1920s, however, dramatic changes in the appearance and behavior of young women made them appear to be rejecting the traditional feminine virtues.

The rise of the social sciences in the early years of the twentieth century created both new fields of study and highly-educated "experts," many of whom

111

were women. These social scientists generally supported the Progressive problem-solving approach to social and economic reforms, and by the decade of the twenties they were also very interested in what we could call gender roles and family dynamics. Although disagreeing on many issues, the new experts played an important part in the partial redefinition of women's roles during the 1920s.

Content Objectives

1. To review the major political, economic, and social trends of the 1920s

2. To know why these changes affected women's lives

3. To learn about the evolution and importance of the social sciences in the early twentieth century

4. To identify the major issues connected with redefining women's roles in the 1920s

Skills Objectives

1. To be able to read social science literature for the messages it contains

2. To understand that all "experts" are influenced by who they are and the times in which they live

3. To infer from the literature the major obstacles to changes in women's roles

When students examine the two interrelated issues in this chapter—women's roles and the influence of "experts" in redefining women's roles—they frequently transfer these issues directly into the present. In general, we do not object because history involves the study of change and continuity over time. As long as the students can understand the issues placed *within* the context of the 1920s, we think that it can also be useful for them to use the knowledge and skills they have gained from this problem as tools to understand the present.

Sometimes their discussion focuses on the central roles women have traditionally played within the family. Over the past thirty years, the number (and percentage) of working class and middle-class families in which both husbands and wives work has increased dramatically. There has, however, been no in-depth examination or reallocation of parenting and housekeeping responsibilities. Some students will raise questions about the quality, affordability, diversity, and even desirability of day care options, questions that are directly related to the issue of working women with young children. Others usually note that religious beliefs, race and ethnicity, and socioeconomic class also influence the definition (and redefinition) of women's roles.

Another direction for a discussion of the broader issues raised by this chapter is to examine the rise of "experts" and their influence on gender roles and behavior. In post–World War II America, psychologists (and, to a lesser extent, psychiatrists) became the new experts for the middle class, especially middle-class women. Of course, various forms of psychological counseling are widely available to young people today in schools, colleges, substance-abuse treatment centers, anger management and conflict resolution programs, and so forth. Sociologists who specialize in gender roles have remained influential, along with social pollsters/trend spotters. Finally, there is a vast market for inexpensive paperback books by experts on gender identity, self-esteem, and relationships between men and women. You may have to prod your students a bit to move them beyond simply identifying and giving examples of the plethora of contemporary experts on sex roles. We find that quite a few students can connect the issues addressed by the experts with current trends in American society; many students will also be able to see that some of the gender issues raised in the 1920s are still important issues today.

The Method

Although the text for the students tells them directly that the new social scientists were influenced by their own frames of reference and the climate of opinion in the early twentieth century, you may need to reinforce this idea. It is especially important for those instances when the middle-class social scientists are concerned with the attitudes and behavior of recent immigrants. Students should not have any difficulty identifying the *message* of each excerpt or the *issues,* such as working mothers, that are revealed by the evidence. They should also be certain, however, to identify the unwritten *assumptions* of each social scientist.

The Evidence

The three categories of sex and sexuality, women's work, and marriage and the family are intended to help students identify and see the interrelationships of the major issues. Of course, there is some unavoidable overlapping among the categories, since changes in one role, for example in sexuality or work outside the home, will obviously affect women's roles in marriage and the family. Comprehending this interconnection will help students to understand why real changes in women's roles were—and still are—difficult to accomplish.

Questions to Consider

Sources 1 and 2 both raise the issue of the new woman's morality, while Sources 3 and 4 apply psychological theory to the question of women's place and roles. Although Groves is a Freudian and Watson is a behaviorist, they both advocate a quite traditional feminine "norm." Students may find the experts in the second category, women and work (Sources 5 through 10), more complex, but the issues are fairly clear: whether married women, especially mothers of young children, should work outside the home; women's basic responsibility for housework (and, by implication, their dissatisfaction and dislike of housework); the reasons why women worked outside the home and the problems they faced; the new role of women as consumers. The final selection of evidence focuses on women's responsibilities within the family: to her husband (Sources 11, 13, and 15); to her children (Sources 12 and 16); and, perhaps, to herself (Sources 11, 14, 15, and second paragraph of Source 16).

You may need to remind students to consider the socioeconomic class represented by the women in Sources 11, 14, and 15 (educated middle class women) and the recipients of the experts' advice in Source 16 (immigrant men and women). Students should also compare the advice aimed at middle-class women (Sources 6, 7, 9, 12, 13, 14, and 15) with the reports of the social workers who visited the working-class families (Sources 5 and 16). The assumption that the primary task of *all* women—regardless of the socioeconomic class of the woman or the gender of the expert giving the advice—was to serve as caretakers for their husbands and children comes as a surprise to many students.

Questions Students Often Ask

Was divorce really so easily obtainable in the 1920s?

As historian William O'Neil has pointed out, the "divorce question" began in the late nineteenth century and came to a peak in the Progressive era. The grounds for divorce were gradually liberalized, women gained slightly more economic opportunities, and the divorce rate did rise. However, divorce was never easy, socially acceptable, or sanctioned during this era.

Were women who did not go to college also "new" women?

Yes, collegiate fashions, hair styles, and the use of cosmetics were widely adopted by young women in their teens and twenties, along with behavior such as smoking, drinking alcohol, using frank language, and casual dating. Young women, including working-class women, were especially influenced by images of women depicted in movies and magazines.

Immigrant women and working class women would not have read social science literature, so how could it affect them?

These women had many opportunities to come into contact with middle-class women through such organizations as the YWCA, social settlement houses, visiting nurse associations, and so forth. Cheap working-class newspapers as well as movie news, short subject features, and radio programs all helped to popularize social science ideas. Social scientific research reports were also widely used in the formation of public policy, such as school curriculum decisions, protective laws for women and children, programs for juvenile delinquents, and so forth.

How important was Freudianism in the 1920s?

Freud visited America early in the twentieth century, but he was relatively unknown outside academic circles until his ideas were popularized in the 1920s. By the mid-twenties, it was nearly impossible to read any mass circulation middle-class magazine without encountering greatly simplified references to the ego, id, Oedipus complex, inferiority complex, or identity crisis. Moreover, some psychologists such as Ernest Groves (Source 3) were greatly influenced by Freudian concepts although they did not identify them as such in the textbooks they wrote.

Was behaviorism really very important in the 1920s?

There were several important psychological concepts formulated or refined in the 1920s. The ideas of W. I. Thomas, John Watson, Harry Stack Sullivan, and Carl Jung were all utilized to some degree by various psychologists in this era. Watson's ideas were, indeed, among the more influential and long-lasting in the United States. Forced from his professorship at Johns Hopkins in 1920 because of unfavorable publicity surrounding a divorce suit, Watson went to work at the New York advertising agency, J. Walter Thompson. During the 1920s, his lectures and publications, especially *Behaviorism* (1925) and *The Psychological Care of Infants and Children* (1928), established his expertise and authority with the middle class.

Was housework really as time-consuming as the sources indicate?

The amount of time devoted to housework depended on many factors: region of the country; rural or urban setting; availability of running water and gas or electricity; standards of cleanliness, etc. Historian Joann Vanek has estimated that women who did not work outside the home in 1926–1927 spent approximately fifty-three hours per week doing housework. As Source 6 demonstrates, preparing meals and doing the laundry were extremely time-consuming chores, even in homes with running water and gas stoves. However, students should not jump to the conclusion that so-called labor-saving appliances drastically reduced the time spent on housework. Instead, as Vanek and others have shown, the development of new appliances such as the vacuum cleaner and electric washing machine actually resulted in higher standards of cleanliness. In 1965, a generation and a half later, women who did not work outside the home averaged about fifty-five hours per week doing housework—two hours more per week than in 1926![1]

Epilogue and Evaluation

The Epilogue tries to highlight the continuing movement of married women and mothers of young children into the work force. It also notes the feminization of both jobs and fashions during the 1950s. By the 1960s, many of these same issues that students identified during the 1920s reemerged: the morality of young women, whether mothers of young children should work outside the home, and a questioning of women's primary roles in parenting and housework.

You may choose to evaluate your students by asking them to write a one-page essay out of class on the assumptions revealed by any three pieces of evidence in this chapter. Or you might wish to quiz your students by asking them to write one or two paragraphs on *one* of the following questions: Based on the evidence, what were the responsibilities of wives toward their husbands? Using the evidence, compare and contrast the experiences of white middle-class and working-class women. Are there any clues in the evidence about what was expected of married men during the 1920s? Instructors with small classes could pair students for research work: some could look at recent books of expert advice on gender roles from the best-seller lists; others could use the 2000 census figures, newspapers, and news magazines for current statistics on working wives and mothers, women's pay compared to that of men, family size and composition, day care issues, and so forth.

For Further Reading

A very provocative and useful primary source for the 1920s is Robert and Helen Lynd's *Middletown* (1929), the classic sociological field study of Muncie, Indiana, in the mid-twenties. Both *Middletown* and *Another Part of the Twenties* (1977) by Paul Carter makes it clear that many people participated only indirectly in Jazz Age lifestyles, yet were affected by the social and cultural changes occurring in the United States. For a study of the youth culture, especially on college campuses, see Paula Fass, *The Damned and the Beautiful: American Youth in the 1920s* (1977). Lynn Dumenil, *The Modern Temper: America in the 1920s* (1995) is the best overall synthesis of the era and the book contributes a good deal to our understanding of women's experiences. David Goldberg's recent overview *Discontented America: The U.S. in the 1920s* (1999) emphasizes the impact of World War I on the major social, economic, and political issues of the decade, but contains surprisingly little information about women's lives.

---

[1]Joann Vanek, "Time Spent in Housework," *Scientific American* (November 1974), p. 118.

Studies focusing on various aspects of the new woman during the 1920s include Estelle Freedman, "The New Woman: Changing Views of Women in the Twenties," *Journal of American History* 61 (September 1974): 372–393. Both William Chafe's *The Paradox of Change* (1991) and Nancy Cott's multiauthored women's history text, *No Small Courage* (2000) offer considerable information about women in the 1920s. Cott's *The Grounding of American Feminism* (1987) is a thoughtful analysis of the impact of modernism on women and women's rights issues. A useful overview is provided by Dorothy Brown, *Setting a Course: American Women in the Twenties* (1986); detailed information about organized women can be found in J. Stanley Lemons' *The Woman Citizen: Social Feminism in the 1920s* (1975).

For information on women's reform networks, see Robyn Muncy, *Creating a Female Dominion in American Reform, 1890–1935* (1991). Economic issues are the focus of Winifred Wandersee, *Women's Work and Family Values 1920–1940* (1981); both Susan Becker, *The Origins of the Equal Rights Amendment* (1980) and Christine Lunardini, *From Equal Suffrage to Equal Rights* (1986) look at the central political questions of the decade.

The emergence and early development of the social sciences are the focus of Mary O. Furner, *Advocacy and Objectivity: A Crisis in the Professionalization of American Social Science, 1865–1905* (1975); Thomas Haskell, *The Emergence of Professional Social Science: The American Social Science Association and the Nineteenth Century Crisis of Authority* (1977); and Donald Fisher, *Fundamental Development of the Social Sciences: Rockefeller Philanthropy and the U.S. Social Sciences Research Council* (1993). Studies emphasizing the role of women in the social sciences include Rosalind Rosenberg, *Beyond Separate Spheres* (1982); Ellen Fitzpatrick, *Endless Crusade* (1990); and Helene Silverberg, editor, *Gender and American Social Sciences* (1998).

The best overview of the new economics, sociology, and political science is in Dorothy Ross, *The Origins of American Social Science* (1991), and the clearest explanation by an outstanding contemporary social scientist is in Robert S. Lynd, *Knowledge for What? The Place of Social Science in the American Culture* (1939). For a wonderful example of the influence of social sciences ideas in the twenties, see Molly Ladd-Taylor's *Raising Baby the Government Way* (1986), a collection of letters from mothers who wrote to the Children's Bureau for advice and the responses they received from the agency.

CHAPTER 7

Documenting the Depression: The FSA Photographers and Rural Poverty

The decline of the family farm and the place of the small farmer in American society was a long and painful process. In the late nineteenth century, the Populist party attempted to restore the imagined "golden age" of the independent Jeffersonian yeoman by demanding nationalization and regulation of railroads, utilities, and other large corporations; more direct democracy, which would shift political power to average citizens; and easier access to money and credit. However, Populist fusion with the Democratic party under the leadership of William Jennings Bryan and the weak regulatory economic legislation passed by the Progressive era presidents accomplished very little for the farmers. After the temporary inflationary effects of World War I, small farmers were excluded from the general prosperity of the 1920s. For many marginal, heavily mortgaged small farmers in the plains and prairie states, and especially for the poverty-stricken sharecroppers and tenants of the South and Southwest, the Great Depression spelled the end of their hopes for an improvement.

The Problem

The unexpected results of the New Deal's Agricultural Adjustment Act, combined with drought, poor farming practices, and foreclosures, turned hundreds of thousands of farm families into landless migrant laborers. The idealistic Rexford Tugwell, like many other members of Franklin Roosevelt's "brain trust," came from a background of urban Progressive reform. The model programs of the Farm Security Administration (FSA)—health clinics, cooperatives, and socially efficient migrant camps—affected only a very small proportion of the displaced farm families. Instead, both Tugwell and FSA Historical Section head Roy Stryker put their faith in educating the general public about rural poverty so as to mobilize support for future, more massive federal intervention. The United States' involvement in World War II put an end to those expectations.

Content Objectives

1. To understand the effects of the Great Depression on the lives of small farmers, tenants, and sharecroppers

2. To learn about the New Deal efforts to alleviate rural poverty

Skills Objectives

1. To learn to "read" documentary photographs

2. To identify the challenges to traditional American values these images portrayed and to understand why they create emotional responses

3. To be able to link the effects of documentary photographs to New Deal reform efforts

Some broader questions that you may wish to discuss with students include the following:

1. Do documentary photographers, filmmakers, and television producers have an obligation to present both sides of an issue, or is it legitimate for them, as social critics and reformers, simply to present the problem as they see it?

2. Is there any place for small farmers in modern America, or have they become economically obsolete?

3. Why have conditions for migrant workers and their families failed to improve significantly during the nearly sixty years since the New Deal first identified and publicized them?

The Method

Because this exercise focuses narrowly on rural poverty during the depression, we balance it with a lecture on urban and small-town unemployment, business and bank failures, and the relevant New Deal programs. A separate lecture covers the important, innovative (for the United States) socioeconomic legislation establishing workers' rights to collective bargaining, a minimum wage, and a standard workweek; the Social Security system; and the Tennessee Valley Authority (TVA), all criticized by opponents as "creeping socialism."

You also may need to help students understand the various ways that photographs provide evidence for the historian. Different kinds of photographic evidence are useful in different ways. The students' own family snapshots, for example, might be used to re-create how people of their race, socioeconomic class, region, and time period lived. Students should be able to differentiate this kind of evidence from documentary photographs, which are generally taken with the intent of stimulating reform.

The Evidence

The photographs have been grouped together to illustrate (1) the destruction of plains and prairie farmlands (Sources 1 through 4), (2) the living conditions of displaced farm families (Sources 5 through 8), and (3) the extreme poverty of tenants and sharecroppers (Sources 9, 10, 12, 14, 16, and 17). The unflattering photographs of the well-to-do plantation owner; owner of the small-town general store, bank, and cotton gin; and mule dealer (Sources 11, 13, and 15) provide a striking contrast to those of the working farm families. The exploitation of black farmhands and sharecroppers is obviously correlated to the more prosperous property owners (Sources 11, 12, 13, 14, and 15). White sharecropper families (Sources 16 and 17) were equally impoverished but usually did not see their common interests with black tenant farmers.

Questions to Consider

The visual impact of these photographs is strong. Most students will be appalled by the devastation of the land and will feel sorry for the families, especially the children. But your students need to move beyond their immediate emotional responses and ask why they feel so sympathetic. The land literally looks dead, unable to support human life as far as the eye can see. Students today are far more environmentally conscious than people in the 1930s were, so you may need to remind them that no one realized how vulnerable the extensive clearing and cultivation had made the plains and prairies. The living conditions and facial expressions of the displaced families, as well as the stoic dignity and will to survive that the photographers captured, will have the biggest effect on most students. In contrast, the plantation owner, small-town entrepreneur, and mule dealer will seem smug, self-satisfied, and uncaring. It should not be difficult for students to link the effects of these photos to support for even such extreme New Deal welfare measures as "the dole"—direct relief payments.

Questions Students Often Ask

Why did these poor people allow their pictures to be taken?
   The FSA photographers were young and sympathetic, and they identified themselves as coming from Washington, D.C., to take photographs to show Americans what was wrong. Most of the farm families hoped that the pictures would stimulate more aid.

How did the photographers know where to go?

Roy Stryker gave them general instructions to travel through certain states or to places where newspaper reports had indicated special hardship. Other than that, they followed their own instincts.

Did any of the photographers get into trouble with the local authorities?

No one encountered any major trouble, although they often met with hostility from sheriffs, local police, or state troopers who were assisting evictions of sharecroppers or tenant families. They also frequently violated local racial sensitivities, because generally, as a group, the FSA photographers were interested in the plight of African Americans. Most of the photographers had never been in the South, and they were struck by (and photographed) "colored" drinking fountains, separate theater entrances, and other signs of strict physical segregation.

Wasn't it dangerous for the women photographers to travel alone in such poor areas?

Dorothea Lange was in her forties and often traveled with her husband, Paul Taylor. When she did travel alone—for example, when she took the famous "Migrant Mother" photo—it was in areas of California where she was already known. Marian Post, however, was younger and unmarried, and Stryker did worry about her sometimes. He advised her not to dress unconventionally and to try to fit in with the local women. She seems not to have been in any really dangerous situations. The other women hired by the FSA later were assigned to documenting the effects of war preparedness on Americans.

Why didn't Gordon Parks, the only African American photographer, take any pictures of farmers?

Parks, a fashion photographer, joined the agency as a kind of intern. Because he had no experience in documentary photography, Stryker told him to look around Washington, D.C., and select his own topics. Parks chose to document the lives of African Americans in the capital city. Stryker may have thought it would be too dangerous to send Parks on the road, but we have no evidence to show that he thought that way.

Epilogue and Evaluation

The Epilogue examines the impact of World War II on the FSA Historical Section and describes its transfer and rapid absorption into the Office of War Information. Most of the young photographers went on to have distinguished careers in the new field of photojournalism. The problems they had illustrated were never resolved and were rediscovered in the 1960s.

Since this exercise seems to engage students' interest easily, we often evaluate it only through discussion. However, it also lends itself to library assignments.

Students may be sent to the library to look at magazines and books of the 1930s to locate and analyze how FSA photographs were used. Alternatively, they may locate World War II documentary photographs from newspapers or *Life* and *Look* magazines, then analyze them for the way they present American soldiers, Europeans, Africans, and Asians.

For Further Reading

T. H. Watkins has written two useful overviews of the depression era, *The Great Depression: America in the 1930s* (1993) which was the illustrated companion book to the PBS series, and *The Hungry Years: A Narrative History of the Great Depression in America* (1999). David F. Berg has edited *The Great Depression*, part of the Facts on File series, which includes eyewitness testimony, editorials, photographs, and other primary sources. An excellent, recently-published diary of a Kansas farm woman's experiences is Pamela Riney-Kehrberg, ed., *Waiting on the Bounty: The Dust Bowl Diary of Mary Knackstedt Dyck* (1999).

William Stott's *Documentary Expression and Thirties America* (1973) is a provocative examination of most forms of documentary expression (excluding film) during the era and an analysis of their common themes. Studies of the Farm Security Administration include Sidney Baldwin, *Poverty and Politics: The Rise and Decline of the FSA* (1968) and F. Jack Hurley, *Portrait of a Decade: Roy Stryker and the Development of Documentary Photography in the Thirties* (1972). A more critical, revisionist study that carefully evaluates Stryker's roles as well as several of the major FSA photographers is James Curtis, *Mind's Eye, Mind's Truth: FSA Photography Reconsidered* (1990).

Lili Corbus Bezner, *Photography and Politics in America: From the New Deal into the Cold War* (1999) evaluates the radicalism of the Photo League, the use of blacklisting, and connects the celebrated exhibit "The Family of Man" with American Cold War concerns. Carl Fleischhauer and Beverly Brannon, eds., *Documenting America, 1935–1943* (1988) includes several nicely reproduced FSA photographs, but is of most value for its introductory essays by Lawrence Levine, "The Historian and the Icon," and Alan Trachtenberg's "Reading the [FSA] File." Also useful is James Curtis, "Documentary Photographs as Texts," *American Quarterly* 40 (1988): 246–252. Bill Ganzel's *Dust Bowl Descent* (1984) juxtaposes 1930s FSA photographs with the author's own 1970s photographs of the same people and places and answers questions of what happened after the depression.

A good starting place for those interested in the work of individual photographers is Penelope Dixon, *Photographers of the Farm Security Administration: An Annotated Bibliography* (1983). Arranged by photographer, this book includes biographical data and lists works by and about the photographers. Karin Ohrn, *Dorothea Lange and the Documentary Tradition* (1980) is a good example of a balanced, analytical study of this photographer and her work. Information about black Americans may be found in Nicholas Natanson, *The Black Image in the New Deal: The Politics of FSA Photography* (1992) which concludes that blacks were more than adequately represented by FSA photographers but that politics greatly influenced which images and how many images were eventually chosen for use. Louis Schmier and Denise Montgomery, "The Other Depression: The Black Experience in Georgia Through an FSA Photographer's Lens," *Georgia Historical Quarterly* 78 (1994) is based on a brief interview with Jack Delano and includes excellent reproductions of his images of blacks in Georgia during the depression. The Library of Congress site at http://www.loc.gov contains FSA photographs in its American Memory division.

CHAPTER 8

Presidential Leadership, Public Opinion, and the Coming of World War II: The USS *Greer* Incident, September 4, 1941

The Lend-Lease Act, which passed the House of Representatives on February 8, 1941, and the Senate on March 11, was probably the single most important event that propelled the United States into involvement in what became known as World War II. This was because, whatever happened in the Pacific, the Lend-Lease Act set the United States on a collision course with Nazi Germany. Once the act was passed and signed, the problem then became how to get Lend-Lease goods to beleaguered Britain with German U-boats poised between transport ships and their destinations. The British could not reassign ships guarding against a German invasion of the British Isles to provide protection of Lend-Lease goods in the North Atlantic. Without that protection, British transport ships would be easy prey for the U-boats. Between January and June 1941, the British lost 756 merchant ships.

Little by little, the implications of the Lend-Lease Act became clear: the United States itself would have to guarantee the safe arrival of Lend-Lease material to Britain, even if it meant escorting convoys and attacking German U-boats. When President Franklin Roosevelt ordered the occupation of Iceland in June 1941 (well inside the U-boats' attack range), it was only a matter of time before incidents leading to war would occur. The USS *Greer* was one of those incidents.

And yet a majority of Americans still believed that the United States should not become involved in a European war. Was the *Greer* incident used by the U.S. government to alter public opinion? Or was President Roosevelt responding to shifting public opinion in his fireside chat of September 11, 1941? Clearly the Lend-Lease Act had provided a potential stage for U.S. involvement in the war in Europe.

124

The Problem

Content Objectives

1. To learn how the United States became involved in World War II

2. To learn how the Battle of the North Atlantic was related to that involvement

3. To learn the role of public opinion in the determination of U.S. foreign policy

Skills Objectives

1. To be able to arrange pieces of evidence to establish a hypothesis

2. To be able to assess public opinion polls and their relationships to governmental policy

3. To be able to determine from varied sources what actually happened in a historical event

On a larger scale, you may want your students to consider the role that public opinion plays in the determination of government policy. For example, are the energy and tax reduction policies of President George W. Bush examples of presidential leadership or caving into various interests? What should the people's role be in the creation of foreign policy when foreign policy itself is such a complex subject?

The chapter also raises some interesting constitutional questions. Article I, section 8 of the Constitution gave Congress the exclusive power to declare war. And yet the president, as commander-in-chief of the armed forces (Article II, section 2) and as chief diplomat (Article II, section 2), could create a situation in which an undeclared war actually might occur. Remember that no formal declaration of war by Congress was passed for either the Korean War or the Vietnam War. The constitutional check here is Congress's control over the purse, to fund such a conflict. Did the founding fathers anticipate such a problem?

Background

The Background section of this chapter begins with the German attack on Poland on September 1, 1939, and concludes with the American occupation of Iceland and the escorting of British supply convoys as far as that island. The concentration is entirely on the European war, so you will have to fill in the important situation in the Pacific. The section is organized in three parallel tracks: the changing war, the United States' reactions, and the shifting of American public opinion. One problem we do attempt to deal with is what appears to be Americans' seemingly contradictory opinion regarding the war. It is our experience that you will have to work very hard to help students understand this. Remind them that no one could predict with certainty what would happen in the future. Thus, could Americans truly believe that they actually could help Great Britain and still stay out of the war? Apparently many did.

The Method

In some ways, this will be the most difficult chapter in the book for many of your students. This is because the evidence has not been prearranged for them. Sources 1 through 11 are the aggregated and published results of several Gallup public opinion polls, arranged in order of their release. These are followed by the reports from the *Greer* and U-652 on the incidents (Sources 12 and 13), in turn followed by two newspaper reports of the incidents (Sources 14 and 15). Sources 16 and 17 are out of chronological order and are excerpts from an earlier memorandum and a conference. These are followed by a German communiqué describing the incident (Source 18). The remainder of the evidence (Sources 19 through 23) is in rough chronological order.

We encourage students to begin by listing the pieces of evidence that will help them answer the question of what actually happened. Obviously Sources 1 through 11 are useless for this purpose and can be set aside. Also, at first glance Sources 16 and 17 would be equally useless, since both actually precede the *Greer* incident. But perceptive students will want to leave them in, since they may help to answer the question of what the U-boat actually did. The remainder of the evidence, even Senator Taft's speech, can help too.

We then ask students to subject each piece of evidence to a "test of believ-ability." Students generally give the two eyewitness reports (Sources 12 and 13) high marks for believability, in part because they tend to corroborate one another. The only serious conflict is Oberleutant Georg-Werner Fraatz's belief that the initial depth charges were dropped by the *Greer* instead of by the British plane. This is an important point.

Clearly various reports of the incident are less accurate. The two stories in the *New York Times* (Sources 14 and 15) omit the actions of the British plane, a crucial omission. So also does the German communiqué (Source 18) omit the plane, thus believing that the *Greer* fired first. And President Roosevelt (who, one assumes, knew all the details concerning the incident) also omits the plane, claiming (as did the *Times*) that Germans fired first. Secretary of the Navy Knox presumably did not tell all he knew either. Admirai Stark's statement, students believe, is considerably more accurate, although his written replies to the Senate committee's questions led students to dub him an "unfriendly witness." Students also say that Taft's description of the incident seems more accurate than Roosevelt's.

Using the two eyewitness accounts as templates, our students then work through the second-hand, third-hand, and other descriptions of the event, finally determining that the U-boat fired on the *Greer* after it had been attacked by the British plane *and* after having been followed for some time (over two hours) and *may* not have known the *Greer* was an American ship and not a British one.

When students finally have reached some form of consensus as to what actually happened, they must repeat the process to answer the second question: whether President Roosevelt used the *Greer* incident to shape public opinion, whether he followed public opinion, or a combination of both. Here the polls will prove useful, but remind your students that they should use the dates on which the polls were *taken*, not those on which they were released. Sources 12, 13, 16 through 18, and 22 may be discarded when dealing with this second question. Show students how to insert the Gallup polls between the rest of the evidence. Roosevelt's press conference and his fireside chat (Sources 19 and 20) will be critical. Was Roosevelt shading the truth? To what end?

The Evidence

There are twenty-three pieces of evidence, including eleven Gallup polls.

Since the students' first question has been dealt with above, the evidence used to answer the second question will be surveyed here. The eleven public opinion polls are the key pieces of evidence. At first blush, students (who are filled with conspiracy theories concerning presidents, the American government and UFOs, college deans, and perhaps even history instructors) will pounce on Roosevelt's clearly inaccurate statements (Sources 19 and 20) and accuse him of trying to push American public opinion into favoring actions that would lead to war with Germany. And, they continue, war surely would have come in the North Atlantic had the Japanese attack on Pearl Harbor not catapulted the United States into the war in Europe as well.[1]

However, if students compare the three polls taken on March 9–14, May 8–13, and August 21–26 (Sources 1, 4, and 6), they quickly see that public opinion already was shifting prior to the *Greer* incident (September 4). After the *Greer* incident, public opinion was considerably more bellicose (Sources 7 through 11). Students who live in states whose poll results are noted in Source 3 will find that piece of evidence fascinating. Can they explain the discrepancies between various states, or why one state (Wisconsin, for instance) was more antiwar than another state (Florida, for instance)? Ohio had a large German-American population, but it also had a large Polish population. How can we account for these poll results? Encourage your students to think about this issue.

---

[1]We do not mention the other conspiracy theory, which says that, failing to goad Germany into war, Roosevelt manipulated the Japanese into the attack on Pearl Harbor, an attack the president knew was coming. Every so often, a student will bring this up.

If public opinion was shifting prior to the *Greer* incident, can your students explain why? Remember that a majority of Americans still hoped that the United States would not become involved. World War I was not so far in the past, and although American casualties had been modest, the principal belligerents had suffered severely (Great Britain lost 20,000 killed at the Battle of the Somme alone).

Questions to Consider

One of our favorite stories is about the teacher who arrived at the social security office to apply for benefits:

"How old are you?" asked the interviewer.
"How old do you think I am?" responded the teacher. "Look at the evidence! I don't answer questions; I *ask* questions."

This section of the chapter asks students questions that will help them to organize the evidence, weigh that evidence, and reach conclusions ("answers") based on that evidence. You will have to help your students a good deal, but be careful not to help them too much. Keep asking questions, referring students back to the evidence or to their text. We have had to role-play here in a number of ways: the person in your state, President Roosevelt, Secretary Knox, Admiral Stark, Senator Taft.

The crucial question, unanswered here, is whether Winston Churchill's memory was correct (it has been found to have been incorrect on a number of points) that Franklin Roosevelt was determined to bring the United States into the war against Germany. What do your students think (see especially Source 20)? What do you think?

Questions Students Often Ask

How did German-Americans respond to the coming of war with Germany?
Some German-Americans joined a pro-German group, called the German-American Bund. But the vast majority strongly supported the United States. One of our grandmothers, who was chased home from school with stones during World War I, was a superpatriot during World War II and wept over the fact that the German people had backed Hitler. Many of her relatives were killed in the war. Incidentally, German-Americans are the largest ethnic group in the United States today.

Why didn't the press, which has been tough on every president from Nixon to Clinton, attack the Roosevelt administration more aggressively for its foreign policy?

Some pro-Republican newspapers, like the *Chicago Tribune,* did so, but not as aggressively as today's media would have done. Prior to the 1970s, the American media were considerably less assertive and investigative. Also, many members of the working press actually liked Roosevelt and enjoyed bantering with him at press conferences (see Source 19).

Lieutenant Commander Laurence Frost had been on the Greer *only thirty-five days when the incident took place. Was his comparative inexperience a factor?*
   No. Frost performed very well. Moreover, some naval officers senior to Frost were passengers on the *Greer* at the time and agreed with his decisions and tactics.

Senator Robert Taft was a leading Republican. Did he have presidential ambitions?
   The son of President William Howard Taft, Robert A. Taft had lived in the White House as a child and doubtless wanted to reoccupy the executive mansion. The closest he came to realizing that ambition was in 1952, when he was defeated for the Republican presidential nomination by Dwight Eisenhower.

How reliable were public opinion polls in the 1940s?
   Polls then and now are only as reliable as the samples of interviewees and the questions they are asked. Compared to today, polling in the 1940s was primitive and not always reliable. Recall the 1948 pollsters who insisted that President Harry Truman could not win over Republican challenger, Governor Thomas Dewey of New York.

Epilogue and Evaluation

The Epilogue returns to the North Atlantic following President Roosevelt's policy shift of September 11, discussing briefly the *Kearny* and *Reuben James* incidents and Congress's amending of the Neutrality Act to allow American ships to transport Lend-Lease supplies. The Epilogue then shifts to the Pacific, briefly detailing United States–Japanese relations from 1929 to Pearl Harbor. The section concludes with former prime minister Winston Churchill's recollection that Roosevelt was willing to enter the war as early as January 1941 but American public opinion was against such a move.
   The evidence in this chapter is complicated. We find it helpful to require students to answer one or both of the chapter's central questions (What actually happened? and Was Roosevelt shaping or following public opinion?) in an out-of-class graded assignment. Throughout the course, we try to keep out-of-class writing assignments to a minimum—or we'd be buried in an avalanche of paper. But there is no question that requiring students to write something prior to class improves both the level of and amount of participation in the discussion. In this chapter, with the evidence both complicated and not arranged for the students,

we find an out-of-class writing assignment to be advisable. Most of our colleagues agree, although they often simply check off rather than grade all the out-of-class writing.

For Further Reading

There is a wealth of studies regarding American involvement in World War II, and of the battle in the North Atlantic. We recommend the following.

Patrick Abbazia, *Mr. Roosevelt's Navy: The Private War of the U.S. Atlantic Fleet, 1939–1942* (1975). An excellent place to start.

Russell D. Buhite and David W. Levy, eds., *FDR's Fireside Chats* (1992). A good primary source with excellent introductions.

Nicholas John Cull, *Selling War: The British Propaganda Campaign Against American "Neutrality" in World War II* (1995). A fascinating study of the British influence on American public opinion.

Robert Dalleck, *Franklin D. Roosevelt and American Foreign Policy, 1932–1945* (1979). A must-read for this chapter.

T. R. Fehrenbach, *F.D.R.'s Undeclared War, 1939 to 1941* (1967). A revisionist interpretation.

Louis Fisher, *Presidential War Power* (1995). A study of the erosion of Congress's sole power to initiate war.

Waldo Heinrichs, *Threshold of War: Franklin D. Roosevelt and American Entry into World War II* (1988). A synthesis, which claims that Roosevelt did not seek war but accepted it.

David Kennedy, *Freedom From Fear* (1999).

Williamson Murray and Allan R. Millet, *Calculations: Net Assessment and the Coming of World War II* (1992).

Geoffrey S. Smith, *To Save a Nation: American Extremism, the New Deal, and the Coming of World War II* (1992).

David Syrett, *The Defeat of the German U-Boats: The Battle of the Atlantic* (1994). An excellent specialized study that will answer many of the students' questions.

CHAPTER 9

Separate But Equal? African American Educational Opportunities and the *Brown* Decision

In 1946, two young African American psychologists with doctorate degrees from Columbia University opened the Northside Center for Child Development in Harlem to provide psychological testing and therapy for African American children. Kenneth Clark, born in the Panama Canal Zone of Jamaican parents, had attended predominantly white elementary and high schools, as well as City College of New York, before obtaining his master's degree at Howard University in Washington, D.C., a highly regarded African American school. While a graduate student at Howard, he met his future wife, Mamie, then a sheltered sixteen-year-old undergraduate from an elite African American family in Hot Springs, Arkansas. Against her parents' wishes, they later married and began a lifelong collaboration and commitment to integration.

It was Mamie's master's thesis on the development of self-identity in African American children and a subsequent grant from the Rosenwald Foundation that led to the famous doll research that was used in the *Brown* case. When NAACP attorneys had difficulty finding established social scientists willing to testify publicly about the negative effects of segregation on African American children, Robert Carter asked one of his former professors at Columbia to recommend some experts. The professor referred him to the Clarks, who had just finished writing about their doll experiments. Carter read the manuscript, became very excited, and telephoned Kenneth Clark. "This couldn't have been better," Carter told Clark, "if it had been done for us."

The Problem

Content Objectives

1. To learn about the changing climate of opinion in the postwar United States that caused many Americans to question segregation

2. To understand the centrality of the *Brown* decision in the African American civil rights movement of the 1960s and 1970s

Skills Objectives

1. To be able to follow the workings of our precedent-based judicial process

2. To learn how to relate the major arguments of a document to the contemporary climate of opinion

This discussion of the desegregation decision may inspire some students to bring up broader issues. Some students may want to discuss (or disagree with) affirmative action at this point. In the 1950s, of course, there was no affirmative action, and the focus was on removing legal barriers to equal opportunities for education and the use of public facilities such as swimming pools. If possible, we like to try to keep the discussion in the time period under consideration by returning to the question of African American identity that proved so persuasive at the time. Depending on your students, this in turn may lead to the broader issues of the roles played by race, gender, and ethnicity in identity or the equally troubling questions of the rights of minorities in a majority culture.

Background

This section is intended to offer a brief review of post–Civil War African American history, with an emphasis on population distribution and migration, as well as on the pervasiveness of racial discrimination in both the North and the South. There is no question that World War II was a turning point for African Americans. Service in the military, growing political power in northern cities, and the formation of African American self-help organizations such as the Urban League and Congress for Racial Equality led to increasingly militant demands for basic civil and legal equality. The U.S. Supreme Court, however, clung to the "separate but equal" precedent set in 1896, in spite of making a series of decisions that had the effect of broadening graduate and professional school opportunities for blacks. During the cold war era that followed World War II, many black and white Americans began to question, and even reject, racially based laws.

The Method

We believe that it is very important for students to understand the slow, careful, precedent-based deliberative process that is at the heart of the American judicial system. Many of our students base their only knowledge of the courts on media spectacles, such as the coverage of high-profile criminal trials (e.g., the O. J.

Simpson trial and the "nanny trial"). But civil courts do not overturn established precedents quickly or easily. In the *Brown* case, the attorneys' briefs for each side were surprisingly short, with the defendants relying heavily on precedent (*Plessy*) and the plaintiffs on social-psychological evidence. The changing climate of opinion is better seen through an evaluation of the *amicus* briefs, the oral arguments, and the decision itself.

The Evidence

You might wish to point out to your students that the first section of the Fourteenth Amendment (Source 1), originally passed to grant citizenship and protections to newly freed blacks after the Civil War, does not mention race or gender, but rather uses the word *person*. Nevertheless, for the first seventy years or so, Fourteenth Amendment decisions usually protected corporations against union activities and state regulation. The amendment was not interpreted to include women until the early 1970s. Students may also need some help in understanding what specific rights might be included under "privileges and immunities"; if necessary, they can review the first ten amendments. Students may need to be reminded that the *Plessy* decision represented the opinion of all seven justices, not just that of Justice Brown who wrote it. Justice Harlan, of course, dissented strongly, and the ninth justice was absent from the hearing and therefore abstained from the decision. Contemporary nineteenth century social Darwinist ideas about black social inferiority are evident through the excerpts from the decision.

The points made in the *amicus* briefs (Source 3) by the veterans, Jews, trade unionists, teachers, and various citizens' organizations are clearly stated, and students should easily be able to explain why each group was sympathetic with the plaintiff's goal of desegregated education. But students may not immediately recall that the context of the U.S. attorney general's brief is in the early years of the cold war, when the United States was directly competing with the Soviet Union for the allegiance of uncommitted peoples, many of whom were Asian or African. Thus, the attorney general argues that America must "set an example for others" by eliminating segregation laws.

Source 4, the oral arguments, shows how the justices first clarified the point that the only reason for assigning students to schools was the race of the children. Next, the plaintiffs rejected arguments about the equalities (or inequalities) of the educational facilities and maintained that segregation itself was unconstitutional; in other words, segregated education could not be equal simply because it *was* segregated. The famous defense lawyer John Davis first tried to break down the credibility of the sociological and psychological experts by suggesting that they didn't understand southern conditions and weren't responsible to southern voters. Next, he used Aesop's fable as a kind of threat: the dog lost the (real) meat he was carrying in order to try to get another piece of (imaginary) meat he saw in the water's reflection and ended up with nothing at all. Thurgood Marshall's often-cited rebuttal focused on children's "natural" tendency toward integration outside school and the artificiality of school segregation. Finally, the excerpts from the *Brown* decision (Source 5) emphasize how much the times had changed since the late nineteenth century and how important education had become in the 1950s. The Court then concludes that segregated public education is "inherently unequal."

Questions to Consider

The questions begin with the Fourteenth Amendment in order to establish the basis for the suit, although most students are probably already aware that the wording of the Constitution and its amendments is very general and thus open to interpretation by the Supreme Court. The *Plessy* decision, especially the Court's dismissal of any notion that racial segregation might be psychologically harmful, provides a direct contrast to the reasoning of the Court in the *Brown* decision. As noted earlier, the *amicus* briefs are very useful for showing the relationship between the contemporary climate of opinion and recent events, such as the veterans' reference to African American soldiers in World War II and Korea and the American Jewish Congress's oblique allusion to the Holocaust. Students should see from questions about the oral arguments that it was important for the plaintiffs' case to move beyond the question of unequal facilities (which *could* be remedied if absolutely necessary to continue segregated education), to the argument that segregation itself was unconstitutional because of its negative effects on African American children. The questions about the decision draw out the Court's belief in the importance of education and their acceptance of the plaintiffs' argument.

Questions Students Often Ask

Who were the men who supported Plessy in his test case and why did they do it?
    Creoles were mixed-race people in Louisiana who were usually very fair-skinned. In New Orleans, there was a Creole community that included many men who were financially secure professionals such as lawyers, doctors, and teachers. In general, these men had not encountered as much racial prejudice as poorer, more rural, often darker-complexioned blacks. However, the railroad carriage law of 1890 divided all people into white or black based solely on racial ancestry, and it was deeply resented by Creoles.

Was Plessy the first test case against the railroad law?
    No, ironically the Creole Citizens' Committee's first effort at a test case (*Desdunes*) failed because the young man, Desdunes, had purchased a ticket for an out-of-state destination before he was arrested for sitting in a white railway car. His case was dismissed when the Louisiana Supreme Court decided in a similar case (*Abbot v. Hicks* 1892) that the separate car law did

not apply to interstate travel because it would violate the interstate commerce clause of the U.S. Constitution. So *Plessy* was the second try for a test case to strike down the law; Plessy's ticket was from one town to another in Louisiana.

Did any women's groups file amicus *briefs in* Brown I?
No, the 1950s saw a postwar turning toward the traditional values of home and family. For middle-class white women, that segment of the population which had earlier spearheaded reform efforts and formed feminist organizations, this meant massive suburbanization, a movement out of the work force, a nearly doubled birth rate, lower age at first marriage, and fewer college and professional degrees. Working-class women had been displaced from their higher paying wartime jobs into service sector and so-called pink collar jobs. Nor were they immune to the societal message that women were first and foremost responsible for home and family. In fact, one of the most striking sections of Gunnar Myrdal's book about the Americans was a list where he compared the stereotypical characteristics of blacks and white women, such as their high visibility, their lack of intelligence, their childishness, and so forth.

Why did the veterans' organization talk about fighting with blacks? Weren't the armed forces segregated?
Even during World War II, when all-black units commanded by white officers were the general rule, both the army and the navy experimented with integration. Furthermore, it wasn't always possible to replace front-line casualties on the basis of race. In 1948, President Truman desegregated the armed forces by executive order.

Why did the NAACP focus on education rather than Jim Crow laws, which must have been very insulting to blacks?
From emancipation and the "field" schools of the Reconstruction era to the twentieth century, education had been a major goal of African Americans. Recognizing education as central to economic and social betterment, such very different spokesmen as W. E. B. Du Bois and Booker T. Washington urged blacks to take advantage of every possible educational opportunity. The NAACP was simply reflecting the priority placed on education by African Americans themselves.

Was Kenneth Clark black?
Yes. His mother moved to New York for better educational opportunities for her two children. Clark was the first African American to receive a doctorate in psychology from Columbia University and the first African American professor at CCNY. (See also the earlier discussion of his life.)

Why didn't the Supreme Court order instant desegregation?

The Court invited the attorneys general of the seventeen states with segregation laws to submit briefs suggesting how to implement the *Brown I* decision. These briefs made it clear that there would be massive resistance and probably widespread violence as a reaction to sudden, complete desegregation. The fear of a major backlash along with the lack of a federal agency or body to implement the decision persuaded the Court that it would be better to allow local and state governments to work out the details of compliance "with all deliberate speed."

Didn't the federal government do anything at all after the decision to help desegregation?

In 1957 there was a kind of showdown between the federal government and the governor of Arkansas, Orval Faubus, who had used the state National Guard to prevent the enrollment of nine African American students in Little Rock's Central High School. Faubus withdrew the guard, but did nothing to control the mob of over a thousand segregationists that surrounded the high school. Very reluctantly, President Eisenhower called out the troops to keep order for the rest of the year. The governor's response was to close down all of Little Rock's public schools for 1958 and 1959. The television coverage of the situation shocked many Americans, however, and polls showed that 90 percent of nonsouthern whites approved the president's use of troops. Civil rights acts, admittedly not very strong or effective, were passed by Congress in both 1957 and 1960.

Whatever happened to the original little girl, Linda Brown?

Linda Brown graduated from a segregated school, grew up, married, and had children of her own in Topeka, Kansas.

Epilogue and Evaluation

Here we tell the story of the slow, uneven desegregation in the South after the *Brown II* decision that basically allowed the states to implement desegregated education at their own pace. In the face of massive resistance in some states and very little progress in others, the federal government finally had to intervene with timetables and guidelines during the 1960s, although subsequent Supreme Court decisions had abolished segregation in almost all public facilities by then. Northern segregation, based on a time-honored practice of assigning students to neighborhood schools, called for different solutions. Urban ghettos, white, often ethnic, neighborhoods, and affluent white middle-class and upper-class suburbs created a volatile situation that resisted any "easy" solutions such as busing.

Many students have strongly held views about racial issues, affirmative action, and the relationships between black and white high school and college students. Rather than quizzing or testing on this material, we like to divide students into small groups. Each group is asked to think through the pros and cons and make a recommendation on one of several contemporary educational initiatives such as community control of neighborhood schools, the establishment of magnet schools in black neighborhoods to attract white students, busing students to and from the suburbs and city, monetary vouchers so that students from poorly performing schools could attend private schools, and so forth. In very large classes, other groups can identify what they think are the major interracial problems at the elementary, middle, high school, and college levels and analyze why such problems exist. When groups report out their "findings," a lively discussion almost always follows.

For Further Reading

In *The Plessy Case: A Legal-Historical Interpretation* (1987), Charles Lofgren analyzes the origins, circumstances, and legal arguments of this test case. Oral arguments before the U.S. Supreme Court for the *Brown* case are available on microfiche and in Leon Friedman, ed., *Argument: The Oral Arguments Before the Supreme Court in* Brown v. Board of Education *of Topeka, 1952–1955* (1969). Two very good selections of documents relevant to the *Brown* decision are Mark Whitman, ed., *Removing the Badge of Slavery* (1992), and Waldo E. Martin, ed., Brown v. Board of Education: *A Brief History with Documents* (1998).

The standard, detailed study of the case is still Richard Kluger, *Simple Justice* (1976). For the broader context of the times but briefer treatments of the *Brown* case, see Hugh Davis Graham, *The Civil Rights Era* (1990), and Andrew Kull, *The Color Blind Constitution* (1992). Philip A. Klinker's *The Unsteady March: The Rise and Decline of Racial Equality in America* (1999) emphasizes the impact of wars and their aftermaths on civil rights progress; John R. Howard's *The Shifting Wind: The Supreme Court and Civil Rights from Reconstruction to Brown* (1999) is good on the changing racial views of the justices. Two related events are covered in Elizabeth Huckaby, *Crisis at Central High* (1980), and E. C. Clark, *The Schoolhouse Door: Segregation's Last Stand at the University of Alabama* (1993).

Biographies of major participants include Bernard Schwartz, *Super Chief: Earl Warren and His Supreme Court* (1983); Edward White, *Earl Warren, a Public Life* (1982); and William Harbaugh, *Lawyer's Lawyer: The Life of John W. Davis* (1973). The lives and research of the Clarks are covered in *Children, race, and Power: Kenneth and Mamie Clark's Northside Center* (1996). There are two recent biographies of Thurgood Marshall: Mark Tushnet, *Making Civil Rights Law: Thurgood Marshall and the Supreme Court, 1936–1961* (1994), a scholarly analysis of his legal career, and Juan Williams, *Thurgood Marshall: American Revolutionary* (1998), a study of his life intended for general readers, which is based on interviews, media reports, and the NAACP records.

Historians have recently begun to be interested in the construction of racial identity of groups other than African Americans. Grace Elizabeth Hale, *Making*

Whiteness: The Culture of Segregation in the South, 1890–1940 (1998) examines the response of southern white people to the rise of a black middle class, the increasing activism of the NAACP, World War II, and the Cold War. Commentaries and reflections on the impact and legacy of the *Brown* decision include essays in a special issue of the *Journal of Negro Education*, vol. 63 (1994); Austin Sarat, ed., *Race Law and Culture: Perspectives on* Brown v. Board of Education (1997); Mark Whitman, ed., *The Irony of Desegregation Law, 1955–1995* (1998); and James Patterson, Brown v. Board of Education: *A Civil Rights Milestone and Its Troubled Legacy* (forthcoming 2001).

For instructors who wish to follow the story further in time, there is Numan V. Bartley, *The Rise of Massive Resistance: Race and Politics in the South During the 1950s* (1969), which concludes that the *Brown* decision was a major catalyst. Both J. Harvie Wilkinson, *From Brown to Bakke* (1979) and Raymond Wolters, *The Burden of* Brown (1994) are good on the backlash against integration and the shift in the Supreme Court personnel and opinions. Harvard Sitkoff, *The Struggle for Black Equality, 1954–1992* (1993) provides a useful, brief overview of this period. Two regional studies of the aftermath of *Brown* are Matthew D. Lassiter and Andrew B. Lewis, eds., *The Moderates' Dilemma* (1998), a study of resistance to school integration in Virginia, and Gregory S. Jacobs, *Getting Around* Brown (1998), an examination of the Columbus, Ohio, public schools.

CHAPTER 10

A Generation in War and Turmoil: The Agony of Vietnam

To some of us now teaching, the Vietnam War era seems like only yesterday. Textbook treatments have begun to appear, and teaching about Vietnam involves a close, sometimes painful examination of our own frames of reference. In spite of the fact that many of us who are teaching at the college level today remember this era vividly, more and more of us are too young to have such searing recollections. And our traditional-age students, who were not even born in 1974, when the United States withdrew from Vietnam, have no firsthand memories at all. Nevertheless, America's Vietnam experience remains at the forefront of our collective consciousness, an only partially healed wound that the past three decades have neither blurred nor erased.

Partially responsible for this phenomenon is the fact that some of our students had parents (or aunts, uncles, or other relatives) who participated in some way in the Vietnam experience—as combatants, war protesters, war supporters, and so on. Also responsible has been the determination of many Americans to let the nation's Vietnam experience influence the government's conduct of foreign policy (recall the continuing references to Vietnam during Operation Desert Storm or during the debate over whether the United States should or should not become involved in, say, Bosnia). Finally, because Vietnam was the last war fought by the United States with the cold war mentality, it is often used as a reference point when discussing contemporary foreign policy dilemmas. Hence, although many college students and instructors have no firsthand recollections of the Vietnam era, that epoch remains for them a concern that has barely receded.

Of course, many colleges today have students older than the traditional eighteen- to twenty-two-year-old undergraduate. At our institution, more than 20 percent of the undergraduate population is older than twenty-five, and that percentage is growing steadily. These students might well make a real contribution to this exercise because they can corroborate much of the material on climate of opinion and frame of reference that is necessary for this problem. Although sometimes these older students feel uncomfortable in a classroom of teenagers, now they can become valuable resources for traditional-age students, which we find very helpful for both us and the older students.

The Problem

To set the context for the students, we trace two major developments: the United States' involvement in Vietnam and the socioeconomic changes in American domestic life. Each development is covered from the post–World War II period to approximately 1970. You might want to use a lecture to fill in domestic politics or some other aspect of this same period. In this exercise, the draft is used as the issue that touches every member of the baby-boom generation.

Content Objectives

1. To learn about containment and our involvement in Vietnam

2. To identify major post–World War II social and demographic changes

3. To become aware of those groups who did not share in the benefits of the "affluent society"

Skills Objectives

1. To compare and contrast oral histories dealing with the same issues and events

2. To be able to conduct an oral interview for historical purposes

3. To understand the concepts of birth cohort and frame of reference

4. To learn how these concepts might influence people's attitudes

On a larger scale, the chapter can stimulate thought and discussion on a number of important, broader issues, such as the following:

1. Traditionally, Americans have prided themselves on their ability to compromise. Are there some issues that should not be compromised? If so, who is to say which ones they are?

2. The protest on college campuses against the war in Vietnam was carried out by a minority of students and faculty members. What rights do minorities possess? Do they have the right to disrupt the activities of the majority?

3. Some people labeled Vietnam protesters traitors. Are people who speak against government policy during wartime traitors?

Background

The Background section is an introduction to the baby-boom generation and the United States' growing involvement in Vietnam. Although we have dealt with some issues relating to the baby boomers in our earlier treatment of post–World War II suburbanization, we have found it valuable to repeat (in a modified way) some of that material, since here we are pointing to the children of the postwar suburbanites as they made their way to colleges and universities beginning in the early 1960s. As for the United States' involvement in Vietnam, today's students find the subject riveting and often ask more questions than we have time to answer. We never forget, however, that our students already have heard at least one version of this story before.

The Method

Oral history *seems* easy to do, and students are generally enthusiastic about it. Many students will "rediscover" some of their relatives and family friends, and this finding presents both an opportunity and a challenge. It is often a good idea to set aside some time before the students conduct their interviews to discuss with them the advantages and disadvantages of interviewing relatives. From the students' viewpoint, some obvious advantages are that they will be able to learn more about their families' experiences and share one small part of their own education with their families. Relatives are readily available and already know the students. Yet students should be aware that many of their relatives are not used to talking with them as adults. Sometimes "messages" are mixed into the interview—how often have we all heard about how hard our parents worked, how far they walked to school, or how strict their own parents were? Other times people want to ignore or omit an unfortunate family situation—a divorce, a prison term, a suicide, a child born outside marriage. Nevertheless, the advantages of interviewing relatives probably outweigh the disadvantages, as long as students are aware of the disadvantages.

The other difficulty many students will encounter in developing a good oral history interview technique is the tendency to write leading or even loaded questions. "All college students were radical war protesters, weren't they?" is a blatantly leading question, but other "closed" questions are more difficult to detect. Also, what is sometimes called a "false dichotomy"—"Were American military leaders in Vietnam brilliant or incompetent?"—is an example of the kind of either/or questions that students should avoid.

Most importantly, students should be urged to begin planning and scheduling their interviews *early*. If time for the reports is an issue, have students work in pairs. To assist students, we have included some instructions for interviewers, a suggested interview plan, and some examples of questions that interviewers might ask. Students should secure written releases from all persons they interview, so we have included three sample release forms (in the Evidence section) that students may alter to fit their (and your) requirements.

Sometimes students have difficulty distinguishing between climate of opinion (which we present through the concept of birth cohort) and frame of reference. One way to see the difference is to understand that one person participates in a collective experience (birth cohort) but also possesses an individual background and personal experiences (frame of reference). Students generally seem to understand individual variations more easily than the more abstract collective experience of a generation, perhaps because they like to think each person is unique. Nevertheless, we think there are enough similarities among these interviewees, in spite of their quite different personal backgrounds and experiences, that students can understand both concepts in working through the exercise.

The Evidence

Students and instructors who used the second edition of *Discovering the American Past* requested that we add some additional interviews, at least one from a veteran who did not experience post-Vietnam adjustment problems and one from a person on the home front who protested against the war in a manner different from that of John. The interviews of Nick and Robyn were added in response to these requests.

Students see immediately that Mike and John come from very different backgrounds. Mike's family was rural, owned their own small farm, and lived in the South. John's family lived in a midwestern academic environment and were upper middle class. Both men noted, however, that their mothers were "liberal" (and somewhat antiwar), and both believed that their fathers expected certain things of them. John stated that he was expected to go to college, whereas Mike believed that he was expected to serve in the military eventually. On one level, for both men college was fun, a place where one met new people and had new social experiences. But whereas Mike attended his local community college in the South, John went to a large midwestern university, where he experienced an intellectual "awakening." Both men dropped out after a year or two, and then their experiences became quite dissimilar.

Mike's account of boot camp is instructive—the dehumanizing aspects of basic training combined with the warnings about how the soldiers might make errors and die in Vietnam. John more or less drifted into the protest movement after he went home to his parents' university town. Each man's initial beliefs were reinforced by his experiences.

Of course, neither man knew much about Vietnam and the Vietnamese people. In fact, they shared the same basic mistrust, even of Vietnamese children. Mike argued that we were helping the Vietnamese maintain their liberty, much as the French had helped the Americans during the American Revolution, but John saw the United States in the role of King George III, suppressing an independence movement for economic reasons. To John, Kent State meant killing students like himself, but to Mike, Kent State meant killing people for expressing the same rights American troops were supposed to be protecting in South Vietnam. For both men, drugs were a means of coping.

Their views about the draft differed dramatically. Mike was fatalistic, believing that sooner or later he would be drafted. John felt relatively safe because of his wealthy background. He knew that those who were drafted were poorer, less well educated, and often black. John's brother obtained conscientious objector status, and when the lottery was instituted and John was denied that status, he was determined to go to Canada if necessary. Drawing a high number made him "safe" again and obviated such a drastic choice. Mike at first viewed protesters as a protected, malcontent minority; John saw them as doing their moral duty. Mike believed returning veterans had done a fine job that no one recognized, but John thought of them as murderers of innocent men, women, and children.

Mike believed in our national leaders and their statements until 1972. He supported both Johnson and Nixon but finally came to believe that we must get out of Vietnam (and thus voted for McGovern). John believed that our national leaders, especially Nixon, were liars and hypocrites. In his final analysis, John firmly believed that the protest movement made a real difference and that it helped expose Nixon (along with Watergate). Mike, in his final analysis, was perhaps more thoughtful, still trying to understand Vietnam, our involvement in the war, and whether any of it was worth the cost.

The interviews with MM, Eugene, and Helen add the perspectives of African American soldiers and a United States Navy nurse to the Vietnam experience. There are similarities among these three people: all grew up in cities, saw military service as a means to further their training or education, and expressed deep distrust of the Vietnamese people. All were very disillusioned by aspects of the war. There are also racial and gender differences. MM and Eugene were very aware of the black civil rights movement and racial discrimination away from the front lines. Helen commented on the perception that American women in Vietnam were either prostitutes or there to find a husband, and she noted the differences in the autonomy of nurses overseas and at home.

The interview with Nick offers a different perspective of the American combatant in Vietnam. Openly unapologetic about his Vietnam experience, Nick wanted the interviewer to know that he respects veterans of the Vietnam War as much as veterans of other conflicts. On the other hand, he shared the other interviewees' contempt for the Vietnamese people themselves. Also, his comparatively smooth transitions into and out of the United States Army cannot be explained by the fact that he preceded the other interviewees to Vietnam, as Mike and MM were in Vietnam before he was and Eugene was only six months behind. Perhaps the fact that he was married had some impact.

Students will have great difficulty with Robyn's interview, even though she is very articulate. The fact that she opposed the war not because she believed it was wrong but because it was being conducted badly at first will be hard for students to grasp, as will the fact that she opposed the war while supporting the soldiers and veterans. This may take considerable explanation on your part.

The photographs are included for their visual impact. Mike's is obviously posed and intended for the folks back home. In full military gear with a sandbagged building in the background, Mike looks mature, serious, and committed—the American fighting man in Vietnam. John's photo is a candid shot taken as he, his brother, and his parents were walking across campus. John's father has short hair and wears a conservative business suit and tie, and John's mother is similarly well groomed and wears a fashionably short skirt (but not a miniskirt). John and his brother have long hair, are much more casually dressed, and are clowning around. This photograph is thus a study in generational contrast.

Students will find it difficult to reconcile the formal photograph of the good-looking, clean-cut, former high school football star MM with his description of himself taking and wearing Vietcong scalps and being demoted seven times. The snapshot of Eugene shows that he is the only African American in the group of marching men, and it is easy to link this racial isolation with his comments about the lack of high-ranking black officers and black-white tension behind the lines. The snapshot of Helen in the operating room reinforces the intensity she still felt when she spoke of being a surgical nurse in a battle zone. The photographs of Nick (similar to Mike's, posed in Vietnam) and of Robyn (at home) add comparatively little.

Questions to Consider

This section tries to encourage students to compare the interviews with one another (four veterans, two protesters) and with the student interviews done in class. This will take some effort on their part and on yours. Remember, however, that we are looking at a *birth cohort* and not at individuals.

Questions Students Often Ask

What was Kent State like at the time?

Kent State University, located in northeastern Ohio, was typical of state universities during the period. The enrollment had tripled during the 1960s and stood at more than twenty thousand students. Many students were from large cities such as Cleveland, but many others were from small towns and rural areas. Fraternities, sororities, football games, and the annual spring mud fight were major forms of entertainment for the students.

Why was the National Guard at Kent State?

Other campuses, such as Harvard and Columbia, were erupted in protest in the spring of 1968, but Kent State was quiet. Then a serious problem occurred in the late fall of 1968, when the Oakland, California, police department sent recruiters to the campus. The Oakland police recently had had major confrontations with the militant Black Panthers, and both the black students' society and the Students for a Democratic Society (SDS) turned out to protest the recruiters' presence on campus. Fights broke out between the protesters and fraternity men, and the Highway Patrol arrested fifty-eight students. In 1970, perhaps reacting to disturbances on other campuses and the fact that radical students had set fire to the Kent State ROTC (Reserve Officers' Training Corps) building, Governor James Rhodes sent the National Guard to the Kent State campus. The guard came directly from six days' service controlling violence in a truckers' strike.

How many women actually served in Vietnam?
About six thousand women served there, in nursing and support-staff positions. None served in combat positions. However, the Vietnam War had an extensive effect on women. Women were concerned about the welfare of fathers, husbands, brothers, sons, lovers, and friends who fought, or might have to fight, in the war, and were very active in the protest movement.

Will there ever be another draft?
It is difficult to tell. There has been a great deal of criticism, particularly by career military officials, of the all-volunteer army. Eighteen-year-old men are now required to register for potential service, which many see as the first step toward a new draft. The final answer to this question probably depends on whether we would ever again need a large conventional army for a conventional limited warfare situation.

Did many go AWOL (absent without leave) or desert during the Vietnam War?
It has been estimated that approximately 1.5 million men went AWOL and approximately 500,000 deserted during the entire period of the war. Approximately 75 percent of the deserters were white and in the lowest ranks of the armed services. About 100 of the deserters were women. During the entire war, only 24 men were convicted of deserting under fire.

Epilogue and Evaluation

The Epilogue ties together the various strands developed in the chapter by following them through time. The amnesty plans and the creation of the all-volunteer army grew directly from the malfunctioning of the Selective Service system during the Vietnam era. The continuation of the protest movement until United States troops were withdrawn, the resignation of Nixon because of his involvement in Watergate, and the subsequent actions of independent Vietnam against Cambodia finish off the story, except for the MIAs (those missing in action). Almost three decades after direct United States involvement in Vietnam ended, there are some signs that the old divisions are beginning to heal. The building and dedication of the Vietnam Veterans Memorial is one such sign.

If at all possible, have your students (individually or paired) report out their interviews. It will not be as time-consuming if you set guidelines for five minute summaries: brief backgrounds of interviewees and three most important points for each interview works well. However, this exercise will be fairly near the end of the term, so you may wish to incorporate its evaluation into an examination question. For example, you might ask students to compare United States involvement in Vietnam with our involvement in World War II (often referred to as "the last good war"). Alternatively, you can ask students which side they would have supported (and why). An outside speaker from the "older" pre-1960s generation might provide further insights, or you might wish to share your own frame of reference and experiences with your class.

For Further Reading

As one reviewer has noted recently, historians and the American public are fascinated with the Vietnam war. "The quality and quantity of publications on this topic appear to far outweigh its importance in American history," she writes," yet skilled and imaginative historians continue to find nagging questions about the conflict they want to answer."[1] Whether or not she is correct about what many believe to be the defining event of the second half of the twentieth century, it is certainly true that the veritable explosion of literature on the era continues unabated. New evaluations of the war, studies of the peace movement, analyses of the military and its service men and women, and first person accounts and memoirs seem to be published almost monthly. The following suggestions provide a starting point for various aspects of the Vietnam war era.

For literature published prior to 1993, consult the series of bibliographic essays in James S. Olsen, ed., *The Vietnam War: Handbook of Literature and Research* (1993). For an overview of the war itself, George Herring's *America's Longest War* (rev. ed. 1985) is still a good place to begin. This may be supplemented with Marilyn Young, *The Vietnam Wars, 1945–1990* (1991); David Levy, *The Debate over Vietnam* (2nd ed., 1995); Robert Schulzinger, *A Time for War: The United States and Vietnam, 1941–1971* (1997); and Larry H. Addington, *America's War in Vietnam: A Short Narrative History* (2000).

There are several good accounts of the peace movement, including the lengthy, scholarly account by Charles DeBenedetti with Charles Chatfield, *An American Ordeal* (1990); the edited collection of essays by Melvin Small and William D. Hoover, *Give Peace a Chance* (1992); Kenneth Heineman's study of the peace movement at American state universities, *Campus Wars* (1993); and Tom Wells's massive survey of the grass roots of the peace movement, *The War Within* (1994). Clyde Taylor, ed., *Vietnam and Black America* (1973) is an earlier collection of protest literature by African American leaders and soldiers. *Peace Now! American Society and the Ending of the Vietnam War* (1999) by Rhodri Jeffreys-Jones also looks at African Americans as well as women and labor groups involved in the peace movement.

---

[1]Anne L. Foster, "Beginning and Ending War: The United States and the Vietnam War," *Reviews in American History* 28 (2000): 630.

There are several studies of dissent and the military. Richard Moser, *The New Winter Soldiers* (1996) argues that dissident veterans provide a new model for peace and social justice, unlike veterans of earlier wars who provided a model for fighting the next war. Robert Buzzanco, *Masters of War* (1996) focuses on inter-service disagreements about Vietnam strategy, and the interaction between civilian policymakers and military advisers. David Hunt, *The Turning* (1999) analyzes the ways in which veterans came to oppose the war.

Lawrence M. Baskir and William A. Strauss, *Chance and Circumstance: The Draft, the War and the Vietnam Generation* (1978) remains the best study of the draft that put more than 2.2 million men in uniform during this years. *Working Class War* (1993) by Christian Appy is based on oral histories of over one hundred combat soldiers. *Bloods* (1984) by Wallace Terry, has interviews with African American veterans; James Westheider's *Fighting on Two Fronts: African Americans and the Vietnam War* (1997) offers a recent overview of black soldiers' experiences. William Hammond, *Reporting Vietnam* (1998) looks at the interaction of the media with the military; Wilbur J. Scott, *The Politics of Readjustment* (1993) is a study of what happened to the Vietnam veterans after the war.

Books critical of American policy decisions in this era continue to appear. These include Lloyd Gardner's analysis of Lyndon Johnson in *Pay Any Price* (1995) and David M. Barrett's evaluation of Johnson's advisers, *Uncertain Warriors* (1993). H. R. McMaster, *Dereliction of Duty* (1997) is a sweeping indictment of both the civilian and military leadership; Frederik Logevall, *Choosing War* (1999) blames both Kennedy and Johnson for decisions that obviated any chance for peace. David Kaiser's heavily documented study, *American Tragedy* (2000) focuses on the origins of what he considers an unnecessary, unwinnable war. Two very important books that are relevant to the disillusionment with our Vietnam experience are Neil Sheehan, *A Bright Shining Lie* (1988) and Robert McNamara's memoirs, *In Retrospect* (1995).

For some specific experiences of instructors teaching about Vietnam and Vietnam veterans, see Renate W. Prescott, "The Vietnam War and the Teaching and Writing of Oral History: The Reliability of the Narrator," *Oral History Review* 26 (1999): 29–46; Michael F. Palo, "Dad, What Did You Do During the War: A Postmodernist (?) Classroom Exercise," *History Teacher* 33 (2000): 193–212; and Patrick Hagopian, "Voices from Vietnam: Veterans' Oral Histories in the Classroom," *Journal of American History* 87 (2000): 593–601.

CHAPTER 11

A Nation of Immigrants: The Fourth Wave in California

Comparing the recent fourth wave immigrants to the massive third wave of immigrants who came to the United States in the early twentieth century, historian Elliott Barkan points out that there are some significant differences. The yearly growth of the recent immigration is not as great as that of the early twentieth century, and the national origins of the fourth wave immigrants have, of course, shifted away from Europe. Nor do the majority of new immigrants enter the country through New York City; over one third of these new immigrants plan to reside in California. Unlike the third wave of immigrants, approximately 30 percent of the fourth wave of newcomers first entered the United States as tourists, students, refugees, or temporary workers. A striking similarity between the two groups, however, is a persistent out-migration in which almost one in five of the new immigrants returned home, much like the "birds of passage" of the early twentieth century immigration.[1]

Throughout our history, successive waves of immigration have had an enormous impact on the economic, political, and social-cultural life of the United States. In this chapter, students use California as a kind of microcosm, or "test case," to examine the origins and experiences of our newest immigrants. In doing so, they are also asked to evaluate the degree to which opportunities still exist for the fourth wave of immigrants.

The Problem

A brief review of the diverse and changing waves of newcomers to the United States established the centrality of immigration in our history. From the earliest settlers from northern and eastern Europe and the seventeenth century introduction of enslaved Africans to the most recent immigrants from Latin America, Asia, and

---

[1]Elliott Robert Barkan, *And Still They Come: Immigrants and American Society, 1920 to the 1990s.* (New York: Harlan Davidson, 1996.)

the Pacific Islands, every group has encountered both opportunities and obstacles in their quest for new lives.

In many ways, California has always embodied the "American Dream" of success. The excitement of the Gold Rush, the glamour of Hollywood, the transformation of arid land into lush agricultural areas, the patriotism associated with the development of the defense industry, and, finally the inventiveness of the Silicon Valley technology companies have steadily drawn new residents, including immigrants, to the Golden State. With the most diverse population in the country, California has also already experienced a serious backlash against the fourth wave immigrants as well as the more complex tensions and sometimes violence *within* immigrant groups and *between* different racial and ethnic communities.

Content Objectives

1. To comprehend the important role that immigration has played in our history

2. To learn about the first, second, and third waves of immigration and the reactions to them

3. To find out the origins of the fourth wave of immigrants and examine their experiences

Skills Objectives

1. To be able to identify the historically relevant points made in the immigrants' life stories

2. To find the "message" these immigrants want to convey, especially about what their goals are

3. To discover the obstacles that the newcomers encounter

4. To evaluate the degree to which opportunity to fulfill their goals still exists for the fourth wave of immigrants

Background

Depending upon the region of the country in which you teach, your students may or may not identify with immigrants. The overwhelming majority of our students in east Tennessee, for example, are a very homogeneous group from old-stock, English and Scots-Irish Protestant backgrounds—in other words, WASPs. Even here, however, there has been a visible Hispanic influx during the past decade, and the employees of the university, Tennessee Valley Authority, and

Oak Ridge laboratories add some ethnic and racial diversity to the area. Thus, for students such as ours, this chapter serves as an introduction to recent national demographic changes as well as a chance to "know" fourth wave immigrants through their life stories.

On the other hand, instructors who teach near the industrial cities of the northeast and midwest may find their students strongly connected to the third wave of immigration. Students on the West coast or in the Southwest may be related to either the "old" Hispanic or Asian immigrants or to the newer (post-1965) immigrants from these areas. Regardless of where you teach, we believe that students can benefit from clarifying their own collective racial and ethnic background(s) before discussing this chapter. This can be done simply by raising hands or, in larger classes, by surveying the students.

One of the broader questions that emerges from a discussion of this chapter is what "success" or the "American Dream" means—historically as well as to the newest immigrants. Unfortunately, sometimes students are more eager to discuss what they themselves think these two concepts mean. Usually, if you can lead the students back to the evidence, they can easily find clues to specific immigrants' goals. From there, students can begin to make some limited generalizations.

The Method

Because personal stories are so interesting, students may be tempted to accept them uncritically. When they find repetitive patterns or themes, such as the strong work ethic expressed by several immigrants, they are obviously better able to generalize. This is just another way of looking for corroboration. Students should also be alert for any "messages" in these life stories.

The Evidence

It will help students if they consider the evidence systematically, as suggested in the Questions to Consider section. Their initial quick glance through all the sources will help them identify the origins and diversity of the Asian immigrants: Vietnamese, Cambodian, Chinese, Taiwanese, and Korean. This can be supplemented by the listing in Source 8. The Hispanics in these selections are all from Mexico, although poet and author Carlos Bulosan, cited in the text, was from the Philippines.

Questions to Consider

Certain themes emerge very clearly from the evidence, such as the belief in hard work (Sources 2, 5, 7, and 9); the importance of education (Sources 1, 2, 3, 4, and 6);

the hardships of poverty (Sources 5, 7, and 11), family and community ties (Sources 2, 3, 4, 5, 6, 7, 9, and 12); and different relationships with whites (Sources 3, 10, 11, and 13). Source 6 presents an example of the "success story" of a third wave immigrant and her family. Families like this provided highly respected models for many of the later immigrants. A few students may also notice the relationships between parents and their children. Although the Questions to Consider do not directly address issues such as the generation gap or Americanization, some of the evidence can easily provide a basis for discussion if students raise these questions.

Students must be careful to limit their generalizations about the degree to which opportunities exist for fourth wave immigrants. Obviously not all immigrants are the same. Urban immigrants have a better chance to start their own small businesses and send their children to school than agricultural workers. However, almost all the immigrants expressed strong family and community feelings, even the teenage gang members in Source 12.

Questions Students Often Ask

Is California really representative of the United States? Isn't it unique?

California is certainly not a *typical* state of the United States, so in that sense it is not representative. Instead, California leads the way; it is the place where national trends first become apparent. This has been particularly true for developments in education, energy problems, and demographic (population) changes in recent years.

What do African Americans think about these new immigrants?

No one would deny that there have been serious tensions between African Americans and Hispanics and Asians. The influx of Hispanics into the Watts section of Los Angeles badly overcrowded the area and eroded the African American political power base there. Another source of resentment was the establishment of Korean and other Asian-owned shops in poor, black and Hispanic neighborhoods. These shops are frequently robbed, and became targets for looters during the 1992 riots.

A lot of these immigrants seem very materialistic? Are they? If so, why?

Owning one's own home and business have historically been important goals for the various waves of immigrants. To a considerable degree, Americans still equate "success" and middle- or upper-class status with property ownership, and so do immigrants. For those who cannot own real estate, fine cars, clothes, and jewelry can be substitutes. Nevertheless, immigrants can be very generous, often sharing their food and living quarters with their relatives who emigrate at a later date.

What are the immigrants' children like? Why don't they rebel against their parents?

Immigrant families are usually close-knit and the children often work out of necessity, to help the family survive financially. Yet, inevitably, the children are "Americanized" by their school experiences and their contacts with California youth culture, such as fashions, language, music, dancing, dating habits, and so forth. This often leads to strained relationships with parents. As we saw in the evidence, some young people also join gangs; there are Asian gangs as well as Hispanic gangs in California.

Epilogue and Evaluation

The Epilogue describes the central issues in the on-going debate over the fourth wave of immigration, and summarizes the most important federal immigration legislation of the last fifteen years. It is clear that an anti-immigrant backlash has been taking place recently in California, yet the census demonstrates that immigrants are continuing to move there. Since this is the last chapter at the end of the term, we rarely evaluate the students, except on the basis of their preparation and participation.

For Further Reading

There are several good, recent overviews of immigration and immigrants, including David Reimers, *Still the Golden Door: The Third World Comes to America* (1985); Roger Daniels, *Coming to America: A History of Immigration and Ethnicity in American Life* (1990); David Levinson and Melvin Ember, eds., *American Immigrant Cultures: Builders of a Nation* (2 vols., 1997); and Leonard Dinnerstein and David Reimers, *Ethnic Americans: A History of Immigration* (4th ed., 1999). Two books focus on the twentieth century: Elliott Barkan, *And Still They Come: Immigrants and American Society, 1920 to the 1990s* (1996) and Reed Ueda, *Postwar Immigrant America: A Social History* (1994) which includes good demographic descriptions of post-1965 immigration. Finally, Donna Gabaccia's article, "Is Everywhere Nowhere? Nomads, Nations, and the Immigrant Paradigm of U.S. History," *Journal of American History* 86 (December 1999): 1115–1134, raises important theoretical questions and argues for a transnational approach to immigrant history.

During the decade of the 1990s, three major publishers introduced new series focusing on ethnicity. Oxford University Press published *The American Family Albums*, eds., Thomas and Dorothy Hoobler, which include illustrations and firsthand accounts from such groups as Cubans, Mexicans, Japanese, African Americans, and so forth. The Twayne series *Immigrant Heritage* edited by Thomas Archdeacon has volumes on people of Asian, Cuban, Japanese, Mexican, West Indian and Southeast Asian (Vietnamese, Laotian, and Cambodian) backgrounds.

Greenwood Press has a series titled *New Americans* with similar coverage, including Koreans, Taiwanese, Dominicans, and Southeast Asians.

The reactions to recent immigration may be found in David Reimers, *Unwelcome Strangers* (1998); David Haines and Karen E. Rosenblum (eds.), *Illegal Immigration in America* (1999); Peter Duigan and Lewis H. Gann (eds.) *The Debate in the U.S. over Immigration* (1998); and Stephen Steinberg, *Race and Ethnicity in the U.S.: Issues and Controversies* (2000). In *Making Americans: Immigration, Race and the Origins of the Diverse Democracy* (2000), Desmond King argues that the choices made in formulating 1920s restrictive immigration legislation helped solidify ideas of racism, especially with regard to African Americans. Elliott Barkan and Michael Le May, *U.S. Immigration and Naturalization Laws and Policies* (1999) is a documentary history; recent analysis of immigration policy include Debra De Laet, *U.S. Immigration Policy in an Age of Rights* (2000); and Nicholas Laham, *Ronald Reagan and the Politics of Immigration Reform* (2000).

The best overview of California history is James J. Rawls and Walton Bean, *California: An Interpretive History* (6th ed., 1993); for more detail, see the five chronological volumes by Kevin Starr, the most recent of which is *The Dream Endures: California Enters the 1940s* (1997). Useful bibliographic essays may be found in Doyce Nunis and Gloria Ricci Lothrop (eds.), *A Guide to the History of California* (1989). The impact of new immigration is analyzed in Thomas Muller and Thomas Espenshade, *The Fourth Wave* (1985) and Bryan Jackson and Michael Preston (eds.) *Racial and Ethnic Politics in California.*

Instructors who wish to teach more about Hispanics should see Joseph A. Rodriguez and Vicki L. Ruiz, "At Loose Ends: Twentieth Century Latinos in Current U.S. History Textbooks," *Journal of American History* 86 (March 2000): 1688–1699. The authors survey eight widely used college history texts, and find little coverage along with distortions in which Mexican agricultural workers are used to represent Latinos of all classes and origins. Jorge Durand et al., "The New Era of Mexican Migration to the U.S.," *Journal of American History* 86 (September 1999): 518–536, argues that the North American Free Trade Agreement (NAFTA) and the Immigration Reform and Control Act of 1986 have changed immigration patterns dramatically.

Good recent overviews include Manuel G. Gonzales, *Mexicanos: A History of Mexicans in the U.S.* (1999) and David Gutierrez, *Walls and Mirrors: Mexican Americans, Mexican Immigrants, and the Politics of Ethnicity* (1995). Background studies specific to California are George Sanchez, *Becoming Mexican American: Ethnicity, Culture and Identity in Chicano Los Angeles, 1890–1945* (1993); Douglas Monroy, *Rebirth: Mexican Los Angeles from the Great Migration to the Great Depression* (1999); and Edward J. Escobar, *Race, Politics, and the Making of a Political Identity: Mexican Americans and the Los Angeles Police Department, 1900–1945* (1999).

For Asians, see Sucheng Chan, *Asian Californians* (1991); Paul Ong et al., *The New Asian Immigration in Los Angeles and Global Restructuring* (1994); Bernard Wong, *Ethnicity and Entrepreneurship: The New Chinese Immigrants in the San Francisco Bay Area* (1998); and Ivan Light and Edna Bonacich, *Immigrant*

Entrepreneurs: Koreans in Los Angeles, 1965–1982 (1988). African Americans are certainly not recent immigrants, but their history provides an important context for racial and ethnic interactions in California. Two recent studies are Rudolph M. Lapp, *Afro-Americans in California* (2nd ed., 1987) and B. Gordon Wheeler, *Black California: A History of African Americans in the Golden State* (1993). A good example of the complexities of racial and ethnic interactions may be found in Leland T. Saito, *Race and Politics: Asian Americans, Latinos, and Whites in a Los Angeles Suburb* (1998), a study of Monterey Park in the San Gabriel Valley.